TALES OF THE TARTAN ARMY

TALES OF THE TARTAN ARMY

IAN BLACK

MAINSTREAM
PUBLISHING

EDINBURGH AND LONDON

Reprinted 2009

First published in Great Britain in 1997 by
MAINSTREAM PUBLISHING COMPANY (EDINBURGH) LTD
7 Albany Street
Edinburgh EH1 3UG

ISBN 9781840181173

This edition 2003

A catalogue record for this book is available from the British Library

Printed and bound in Great Britain by
CPI Cox and Wyman Ltd, Reading, RG1 8EX

*For my clan, my country
and my comrades in arms*

Contents

1: The Night We Were Beating Brazil

'Get us a cubalibre, Wullie.' 'Aye right. Heh Amigo, two cubalibres.'

A street café in Seville, three quarters of an hour to the kick-off, five minutes walk to the ground. The enterprising café owner has laid hands on hundreds of plastic pint glasses and is running to and fro quietly making a fortune.

'We didny stop at Derby this time, eh son?' says a guy sitting across from me. He is gazing around with a satisfied air. The place is thronged with every known variety of tartan, sticking to sweating bodies. It is about 95°F, unbelievably humid, and there are 200 people in a space meant for 20. You can taste the adrenalin in the air.

'Brazil', the word is like an incantation, half a dozen heads turn. 'Who huv they goat? – Apart fae thur team. Name me a famous Brazilian who disny play fitba! Ye canny, kin ye? See whit a mean? We're gonny tank them!'

His fist comes crashing down on the table.

'Zi-co's a barrel, Zico's a barrel of shite, shite, shite.'

Lumpy George is gazing at this old guy with a kind of awestruck disbelief when he catches my eye and I realise I am doing the same. We burst out laughing. The old guy smiles.

'Aye awright, boys. Ah know, ah know, jist whislin' in the dark. But maybe this time we'll play like we can, we'll show them yet, eh? Did ye see Robbo's free kick against New Zealand? Ma heart near burst, I was that proud. Ah've watched us learnin'. Ah wis in Germany when we shoulda beat Brazil. We ootplayed them. Wee Billy wis desperate unlucky no tae score. Ah missed Argentina, thank Christ. She wisny well an ah couldny go. But this time we might be ready an ahm here tae see it. Ye goat digs okay? Ahve a big room if yer stuck.'

'We're okay,' George tells him. 'Thanks a lot though.'

In front of us Big Andy spits out his cubalibre and says to Wullie, 'This is fuckin gin!' I lean forward to explain that they make cubalibres with gin in Seville unless you ask them not to, having made this mistake less than an hour ago but Wullie says, 'Leave this tae me.' He gets out his phrase book and stands at the bar, lips moving silently. The barman appears, Wullie holds up his glass and shouts, 'Why you give us gin?' Lumpy George – who lost a bet that you could sleep outside in Spain without being bitten by mosquitoes or attacked by pro-Argie fanatics – sprays his beer all over me, down his nose, eyes streaming – 'Let's go before these guys are the death of me.'

We stand outside in the moist air, finishing our pints. Brazilians and Scots stream past in their thousands, eyes glittering, bodies taut 'SC-O-O-OTLAND' 'BRAZEEL'.

Brazilian drums are booming, whistles screaming like a thousand mad referees. In the near distance the skirl of the pipes raises the hair on my neck. Round the corner swings the Inverness division of the Tartan Army – Builder John, his wife Anne, Mac the piper, the Maryburgh Monster, seen in public (by me at least) for the first time without a chestful of sick. Sweeney and Mahoney – a pole each – hold high the message 'Spanish Sheets Make Good Banners' the worlds's first existential flag. George and I fall in behind, voices raised in song, scarves held high, Scotland jerseys a badge of pride, grinning and shaking hands with the canary-shirted Brazilians – '*Buen suerte*, pal – good luck – you're gonny need it – ah hope!'

We're in the ground – behind the goals. The noise is deafening. Polite, conservatively dressed Spanish men and women smile bemusedly at us. One of the Spanish guys is wearing a Celtic scarf. I point 'Celtic?'

'*Naw señor – Real Betis.*'

'*Real Betis – aqui en Sevilla?*'

'Yes *señor*, here in Sevilla – *como Celtic en Escocia – la bandera, si?*'

'Yes, like a Celtic scarf. *Si. Si.*'

'Is that how they say no? *Naw* – just like us – aye, no man is an island, eh!' says Mahoney. 'Tell him we're gonny gub Brazil, Wee Man.'

The game is about to start, every half-back in Scotland is playing, Stein wants to keep the score down. Twenty minutes in Narey lashes it past the Brazilian defence and goalie. It's in! It's in! George is screaming 'We're beating Brazil, we're beating Brazil'. Mahoney is dancing round and round with the Real Betis supporter shouting, 'Ah telt ye, ah telt ye,' in his ear. The Spaniard is laughing, sharing our joy.

The Brazilian drums stutter, the beat staggers, almost dies, picks up, intensifies. The left hand stand is a yellow wall of sound. Boom boom, BOOM, boom, boom boom, BOOM, boom. On the field Scotland are stroking the ball around, beating the Brazilians at football for Christ's sake. The Spanish people around us begin to clap rhythmically. It sounds like a dance beat. My friend explains – '*La Sevillana*, your men – very good.' I later learn that this clapping is high praise indeed, accorded to very few.

Nearly half time. Free kick to Brazil – not a foul, but what the fuck, Roughie will get it. Zico. Crack. Net bulges. Rough rooted to spot. Archibald stares at him with a look that would wither trees. He mouths 'Ya fuckin tube'. One all. Half time.

We lost the second half 3–0. A sentence that encompasses troughs of despair, loss of belief in God, George, a renowned purist, screaming 'Whack him, whack him' as Socrates steered the ball effortlesstly all over the field, highs of wondering appreciation as Brazil played Brazilian football – football as it should be played.

At the end, as we're leaving the ground the two streams of supporters converge on the exits. The Brazilians are drumming faster than ever but keep casting wary glances at us. They have been reading in the Spanish papers about the '*Hinchas Escothes*' and we do take a certain pride in looking like a barbarian horde. George and Andy start to sing along with the samba beat. 'The best team won, the best team won.' Soon all of us are at it. I have never heard losing Scottish supporters sing this before. I have never felt like singing it before myself. We all grew up a wee bit that night.

As the two lots of fans merged there was much hand-shaking, hugging, backslapping, swapping of scarves and jerseys, offers of drums, drinks. I spot a Brazilian drinking a can of McEwans Export. Then we hit the bars.

Seville was a carnival that night. Scots and Brazilians and Spaniards danced in the streets till past the dawn.

Mac the piper learned to play the samba. We played 20-a-side football inside a huge café, with laughing waiters joining in.

Big Andy proposed to Anne Marie and she accepted. The café owner gave them a bottle of champagne. We moved from bar to bar as the beer ran out. George and I did a Butch and Sundance into the river, but it was only about a foot deep. One of the police who helped us out was laughing so much he nearly choked himself. At 8 a.m. a whole barful of us made a solemn vow to meet again on this spot on Fair Friday, 2001. If you're ever going to have a carnival, have it in Seville.

As we boarded the Malaga train, Builder John is muttering 'Ach well, if you're going to get beat, you might as well get beat by the best.' Big Andy puts on his Bogart face and says to Anne Marie, 'We'll always have Seville.' She says, 'Imagine telling our weans we were there – the night we were beating Brazil.'

2: The Kilt Police

Our first and last encounter with the Kilt Police was in Malaga, where we'd based ourselves rather than going to any of the coastal holiday towns, because the accommodation was cheaper and so was the food and beer. I'd been the scout and I'd got there two days before everyone else and found us a great big apartment with about ten rooms in a block which enclosed a superb garden, tenderly cared for by Tio Pepe and Tia Maria, which means Uncle Pepe and Auntie Mary. Everybody in the block called them Tio and Tia so we just did it as well, except we added Pepe and Mary. I'd had to negotiate the price with Uncle Pepe and he knew all about hooligans, football and otherwise. Because of the behaviour of holidaymakers in previous years, not just Scots, but English, Dutch and German, he stuck out for a deposit of £500. He was unimpressed with the fact that we were Scottish rather than English and he didn't even like the Spanish football team. All of my negotiating techniques were failing and I didn't have £500 in cash and no immediate possibility of getting it. This was in 1982 and getting money out of a bank in Spain was a bit like trying to talk yourself into Fort Knox while wearing a bowler hat and calling yourself Oddjob.

He was quite impressed with my Spanish, which I'd been

practising for months, and he corrected my pronunciation and taught me a couple of localisms as well as telling me about local people. While we were talking about politics, I mentioned that I had seen a statue of a Scot in Madrid and that there was a statue of a Spaniard in Glasgow. The statue I'd seen in Madrid was of Sir Alexander Fleming and Uncle Pepe knew all about it. He explained that since Fleming discovered penicillin, bullfighters no longer automatically died a horrible death if they suffered a *cornada* – a deep horn thrust. He told me that the one I'd seen in Madrid had been erected by the friends of a famous bullfighter and that there were dozens more all over Spain, all put up by bullfighters who were still alive because of him.

I told him of the statue of Dolores Ibarruri which stands beside the Clyde in the Broomielaw. She was an anti-Franco heroine of the Civil War, known as *La Pasionaria*, the Passion Flower, for her fiery oratory and her courage. She stands there with her fists defiantly in the air and on the plinth it has a bit from one of her most famous quotes which includes 'Better to die on your feet than to live on your knees'.

I was trying to tell him this in my far-from perfect Spanish when he said, 'A moment,' and nipped into the next room, shouting for his wife. He came back with her and said 'Tell her what you told me'. Tia Maria, it transpired, had actually met *La Pasionaria* in Valencia before she went into exile and had worked for her on her return. She was still alive at this time but Auntie Mary said that she was pretty old. (She died in 1989, aged 94.) Auntie Mary and Uncle Pepe were pretty impressed with Glasgow for having put up a statue to her and after we'd talked about the International Brigade and the Scots and other nationalities who had died fighting for the freedom of Spain and had a glass of wine, the financial situation became immediately much brighter.

They both insisted that no deposit was necessary and I found myself insisting that they take some money. We settled for 20,000 pesetas, about £100 and still quite a lot of money in Spain, but I had to force them to take it. Then it was the ceremonial presentation of the receipt and then the *paseo* round the neighbours' houses to be introduced as 'The Communist Scotsman from Socialist Glasgow'. I'm not a communist, though

I have been, but I didn't like to spoil their pleasure. The story of the statue had to be repeated several times, getting more elaborate each time. He didn't knock at one intricately carved door, a Dr something, and when I asked Uncle Pepe said simply '*Fascista*'.

Much good was to come from this meeting for me and the rest of our squad because Uncle Pepe took us to a couple of the Spanish equivalent of working men's institutes and we were always welcome there. The beer was dirt cheap and the crack was great. He took me out to one that afternoon and it was there that he told me of the '*Hinchas Escothes*', the Scottish fans, whom he had seen upending a guy in a kilt and removing his trews. We were to hear more of them later.

The troops drifted in over the next couple of days, Bodyswerve and Big Andy stopping everyone's hearts by arriving in a police car. They'd asked the cops for directions and they couldn't understand a word they were told, so the cops just brought them round. Andy gave them each one of his scarves, of which he has dozens, and that was us fixed up with the authorities as well because the police gave Andy a card and told him to phone them (with someone with him who could speak Spanish, the polis smiled) if there was ever any bother. The only time we did phone them was to invite them to the pre-game party on the Tuesday night of the New Zealand game. They turned up in jeans and one of them got off with the woman that Andy was trying to chat up. He was not a happy pixie, which for Andy means giving a fair impression that the biggest thunderstorm in the world is about to take place. George said, 'She hadn't a clue what you were saying,' and Andy snapped, 'Aye, but she knew what I meant.' This was so patently true that everybody burst out laughing, including Andy. 'Yes,' said George, 'she was tried and found wanton, Andy, but not by you,' and he nodded to the happily entwined couple in the corner.

We had met a few Kiwis and some of them were there. Someone then said that in Scotland Kiwi was a boot polish and one of the New Zealanders said 'That will be what the Kilt Police are using'. He then explained that there was a ten or 12 strong bunch of lads going round checking people in kilts for knickers and if they found any they upended the offender and boot-polished his genitals, carrying off the trews as trophies.

Our crew, true Scotsmen to a man, looked smug and secure. 'If they pick on me,' said Andy, 'I'll give them my impression of a tartan lampshade,' and he jumped over and did a handstand against the wall. 'This is the giant, hairy bollocks model of the tartan lampshade,' said George, as Andy is not under-equipped. The polis who wasn't necking with the girl asked me what was going on and I explained. He said, 'Not wearing clothes under your kilt is probably against the law here,' but he thought that this Scottish custom, and the Kilt Police, were very funny. He said something to the two in the corner. They laughed and the girl definitely renewed her interest in Andy at that point. His mate looked a little put out but he laughed as well and after a few beers we gathered ourselves together for the game, which turned out, unsurprisingly, to be one of two halves, and we only liked one of them.

The Kiwis asked if they could walk up with us and we agreed. There must have been about 20,000 Scots in Malaga and the place was buzzing like a billion bees. As eye met eye and we girded our loins, something the Kilt Police were going about undoing, Mahoney, there for the first time with his new mate Sweeney Todd, said prayerfully, 'Surely we can beat New Zealand'. There was something in the way he said 'New Zealand' that stiffened the backs of the Kiwis and George delivered Mahoney's first lesson in Tartan Army tactics. 'Never underestimate Scotland's opponents. That is the crime of Hubris and when Fate hears it, she leans down and sticks her finger up your arse.' The Kiwis were smiling and George went on, 'These Kiwis might be from a few benighted islands on the doup of the world, with no culture but the few shreds that remain from the people they stole the islands from, and who have never kicked a ball in the World Cup, but they produce a team of iron-hard ruthless bastards who beat everyone in the world at rugby, their real game, and we will show them some respect!' And his hand hit the table like a gunshot. He locked gazes with one of the New Zealanders who was giving him the thumbs up and went on, 'Then we'll put ten past them.'

Then we poured out onto the street roaring 'Give us ten, give us ten, give us ten,' laughing like maniacs, carrying the Kiwis along. We marched up behind the big banner that said, 'Let's polish off the Kiwis,' through a mass of Spanish people cheering us. The *Hinchas Escothes* had made their merry mark and we had many friends wishing us well.

The first half was a dream for us and a nightmare for the other side and our new mates were looking a bit grim when we went three up. George was joshing them along, 'You're doing well, but that wee man Strachan is destroying you.' It was about 90°F and the players were lashing buckets of sweat when they went in at half time. We later surmised that Stein had told them to slacken off to save energy for the Brazil game but when Danny McGrain gifted the Kiwis a goal with a terrible passback and then ten minutes later one of them went through on a long ball, a mile offside, and nearly burst the net behind Rough, things got a bit tense. 'Yeah,' said Mark the big Kiwi to George, 'here comes that Fate lady with her finger out,' and they all started yelling 'Give us ten!' You couldn't help laughing.

Kidding and swanking is okay when you're winning but the pain went away when Robertson chipped in an absolute beaut of a free kick and then Archibald finished them off with a header from a Strachan corner. We'd won our first game but the Kiwis had their heads held high. We explained to the Kiwis that the Army always pays for the beers when we've won (which isn't all that often) and we set off to hit the bars.

Just a couple of hundred yards towards town we came across a wee lad of about 11 or 12. He'd lost his dad and he looked as though he'd been crying. His dad, sensibly enough, had given him a piece of paper with his holiday home address in Torremolinos and that of a bar only five minutes away, to which the first Spanish guy we spoke to gave us precise and accurate directions. He was a nice quiet boy in a MacGregor kilt and it transpired that he wasn't just crying because he had lost his dad, but because he had been set on by the Kilt Police, and suddenly they weren't funny any more. 'They've rubbed black stuff right in, and it's all over me,' he sniffed, 'and they've taken my pants.'

'That is not funny and it isn't right,' said Anne. 'Doing that to a boy that age, that's not a joke, that's cruelty.' Builder John, her husband, was enraged, as they have boys of their own. He and Anne and George took him into the first bar we came to and Anne produced moist tissues and cream and we got some butter from the counter. Anne sat with us as John vanished into the toilet with the boy to explain how to get rid of boot polish stains. 'He's a bit shy and embarrassed,' said John on returning, 'but he's not physically hurt. He told me that those bastards made jokes about the size of it.' Anne was beside herself. 'It's just not fair,' she kept saying and if any of the Kilt Police had fallen into her hands at that moment they would have been the worse for it.

Mahoney and Sweeney had gone to fetch the boy's dad, whom they'd found by shouting the boy's name in the bar he'd designated and just as wee John came out of the toilet, big John appeared and clasped him in his arms.

The Tim Twins hadn't told big John what had happened, just that his son was with us, because the boy had to make his own decision what to tell his dad. He sat at the table with his Coke and told his tale without a tremor, how he'd got separated when he thought his dad was behind him going to the loo. He'd figured that someone had spotted his trews in the toilet and said that they just pounced on him outside. 'They weren't very nice, Dad,' was all he said about his ordeal. Big John, who is bigger than Andy, which means he must be about six feet six inches, could see that we were a bit grim-faced and one of the Kiwis told him about the Kilt Police. He laughed at first until he realised that it had happened to his son and then he asked 'Where can we find them?' George noted the 'we' and it turned out that John's two brothers and sundry others were with them on holiday. I never met them but Andy told me that one of them was bigger than John.

We walked back down to the centre of town with wee John jumping around us, oblivious to the celebrating hordes, asking, 'Are we going to get them, Dad?' I helped John to phone his wife and tell her what was going on and he came out of the phone box smiling broadly. 'The Kilt Police are in right trouble now,' he said, 'the women are on the way.'

We established ourselves in a long, old-fashioned bar with giant hams hanging from the ceiling, one Uncle Pepe had recommended, and got on with the celebrating and the sampling of the 47 different kinds of dried pig that they had, not to mention the beer and the wine. The Kiwis kept trying to pay, but we insisted and eventually Mark and his mate got up and left saying they'd be back in a bit. Ten minutes later they were back. 'We've found them, at least some of them,' said Mark. 'We've found the Kilt Police, we're paid up.'

John's wife, wee John's mother, arrived about two minutes later with about a dozen other women from their hotel, leaving their men outside. Once it was established that wee John was okay, she thanked us in that brusque Scottish way that quietly means something like, 'All that I have is yours for the asking and me and my blood are behind you to the death.' The Kiwis told her they'd show her where the Kilt Police were and everybody left but George and me, as we were waiting for Aunt and Uncle, whom we'd promised to meet there.

This is Andy's description of what happened. 'You should have seen them. The Ride of the Valkyries wasn't in it. Storming along the street they were, and by the time we got to where they were there were hundreds of people. That's where I met Anne-Marie.' Only Andy could pick up a girl in the middle of a proto-riot. 'She was wearing a Scotland top and drinking San Miguel by the neck,' said Andy, establishing the qualities that have kept them together for nearly 15 years.

'Anyway, Mrs MacGregor confronted the guys. They had a great big sign propped up against the wall that said, "Debriefing Centre", quite funny really, but she was for none of it. Wee John was produced and he recognised a couple of them. She started to talk and one of them started laughing at her. Big John just reached over and picked him up by the hair. It was really long but only his toes were on the ground. He's a big guy, that John. The upshot was that we all left and wheeched them round the corner into a square. The kilt guys were really scared by now as there were hundreds of hands against them.'

Andy went on, 'Anne said, "Get them to do it to themselves," and one of their sporrans had boot polish in it. Under serious threat from John and a few others they all had their hands up each others kilts, rubbing away. If it had been a movie it would have been totally shagging hilarious. When they had done, there were dozens of Spanish people there, laughing and laughing. I started laughing as well and so did wee John and his Dad, but the Valkyries weren't finished.

'"Right John," said Mrs MacGregor, "take their kilts, they don't deserve to wear them."' Andy was laughing like a drain by now. 'So they got a hold of them and took their kilts off, every one. "That looks like the last chicken on the shelf at Safeway," said Mrs MacGregor to the one who had given her snash in the café. The crowd roared, though Christ knows how they translated that into Spanish, and Miguel and his mate arrived with some uniformed polis.

'They got flags and tablecloths wrapped round them and the polis took them away in the van. John had to collect up all the kilts and take them round to the polis station.'

The group were released without being charged and the only arrest during the whole of the Mondial in Malaga was a guy who demonstrated to a Spanish woman who asked him what a Scotsman wore under his kilt. He wasn't charged either, though they kept him in for the night.

The Kilt Police disbanded at that point, though we still see a couple of them at the game now and then. One of them is called Safeway, and now you know why.

3: Alcoholism versus Communism

Most of us spent the Saturday after the Brazil game either sleeping on the train back to Malaga or trying to find comrades who had gone missing in action during the best street party that the Tartan Army was ever part of. Half a dozen of us had caught the early train and by the evening we were in one of our usual haunts, the restaurant contained in *El Corte Ingles*, a major Spanish department store chain.

It means 'The English Cut', and we had had major problems with getting some of the guys to go in but it is a really great shop with staff who take you to where the stuff you want to buy is and then make sure that you get exactly what you want.

We thought it meant 'The English Court' at first and one of the staff, whom someone had told about it, dubbed our meetings there *'El Tribunal Escothes'*, which does mean 'The Scottish Court', and it was there that we hashed over the games and got the Spanish crack from the staff. By this time *El Ejercito Tartàn* was mega-famous in Malaga because not only had we been on the telly both before and after the game in Seville, but they had also been showing scenes from the parties and doing interviews with the participants. The Brazilians were adamant that we were the best supporters in the world while we were equally adamant that they had the best team and that their supporters weren't half bad either. There were 30,000 supporters in Malaga by this time, with friends and families, everybody keen to give the lie to the canard about Scottish meanness, and the people in Malaga thought we were just great, which we reciprocated.

A couple of the guys had got Spanish girlfriends (no easy feat) who worked in the Court, as we called it, and because of that we spent a lot of time there. The fact that it was one of the few bars or restaurants in Malaga to be fully air conditioned and that they had a cover charge of something like £5 which meant that you could stay there all day eating as much as you liked from a huge and delicious buffet, not to mention that some of the troops were getting wee Spanish delicacies and drinks on the sly from the girls, helped a great deal, too, but it was just a great place to chill out and to make plans. It must have been the only place in Malaga where we didn't sing. It was great seeing the shock on the faces of the suited-up businessmen when they came in and saw 60 or 70 of us all over their restaurant but what was even nicer was the smiles when they recognised who we were and the fact that they talked to a beer-soaked bunch of headbangers with enthusiasm. They love people who are enthusiastic, particularly people who are enthusiastic about football, and we got to know a few of them quite well.

One of them had produced an English-speaking priest for the Tim Twins that Saturday and they were planning a recruitment drive for Mass for the next morning with his help. 'And will you pray for the Scots, Father?' asked Sweeney. 'And for the Russians, my son,' said the priest. 'But the Russians are Godless communists, Father!' said Sweeney, who has a simple and fairly religious way of looking at things. 'All the better reason that we pray for them. Don't you agree, Tomas?' I don't think Mahoney had seen the inside of any religious institution for quite some time and he's a rabid Trot, but he wanted to support his pal, and he was nodding vigorously. 'Yes, Father, pray for the Russian team.' 'Only for their souls, Tomas. Only for their souls. We want Esocia to win this one,' said the priest with a smile. 'And we'll see you at confession,' he continued to Mahoney with a touch of steel in his voice, recognising a Godless communist when he saw one. 'We'll be there, Father,' said Sweeney.

The question of proper dress, a very Scottish Presbyterian one, was raised by George and the priest looked quite taken aback at talk of collar and tie. 'Come as you are dressed now. We will get more of our people if you wear your tartan, your keelts. During the *paseo* tonight we will be telling people that the *Escothes* will be there. You will be helping to bring people to God.'

The Darkie, who thinks that the best way of bringing people to God who are not of his narrow-skulled, mean-souled brand of Protestantism, is to torture them to death, had had enough, but he didn't say anything. This is a man who thinks that the Orange Lodge is a branch of effete wimps, religious-wise, and that the Wee Free are getting a bit nearer The Answer but aren't anywhere close as yet, but he still didn't say anything. This was because Andy had stuck his fingers right into The Darkie's ears and was pressing quite hard. He didn't do it to shut off the words that the priest was saying but as he said after he'd hustled him out of the door 'I could see he was going to insult the priest there, and we don't want to be bothering our hosts with advertising that one of us thinks that Hitler made a mistake not including the Catholics, eh?'

Tam and Sweeney, meantime, were talking about the *paseo*, this Spanish custom of swanning around, dressed not just to kill, but to kill at a thousand yards, with the priest, because they fancied doing it. George explained, as George does, that as well as being a mating and matching ritual, it is also an exercise in displaying what you've got, and of seeing what the others of your peer group have managed to extract from the system.

Billy the actor, after listening to George for five minutes, said, in a pretty good version of George's voice, 'Look chaps, I'm afraid this man's vocabulary is on the Pat and Mick, the sick. I do believe it has elephantiasis. It has swollen to the point where a new name is called for. I think we should call him the Elephantiasis Man.' So we did. For days, and it drove George crazy. He's not going to give Richard Gere any problems in the good looks department, and at that time he was covered in lumps and bruises as well as having shaved his head, not a common thing to do in those days, so he got a bit upset. 'Ignorant louts,' he said, proving Billy's point. It might be short but 'lout' is not a word much used in our daily lives as footsoldiers. It's a bit close to home, which George knows perfectly well, of course. 'Pantaloons, jackasses and tomfools,' he continued 'why don't we do our own *paseo*?' The Spanish people present thought this was a great idea and in five minutes everyone in the restaurant was talking about it. 'It is of course a sexual ritual as well,' George said, and, intercepting a frown from the Father, went on 'though not an occasion for the exchange of bodily fluids,' at which the young priest blushed slightly. George noticed this and went on, a tad louder. 'No, bodily fluids play no part in the *paseo*. Bodily fluids are for retaining during the *paseo*. Bodily fluids –' at which point the priest stood up and said to the Tim Twins in a slightly strangled voice 'See you soon', and hastily hurried away.

The businessman who had introduced the priest to Tam and Sweeney thought that this was hilarious and nicked off to cancel his appointments for the rest of the day, making a joke in Spanish to his pals on the way out about what the priest was off to do. I know all the sweary and sex words in Spanish as I learned them first, and I am not going to share the slang term for masturbation at this point, though I did at the time, and for the following couple of days it was used frequently by everyone when the young priest was anywhere near.

Meanwhile *paseo* fever was growing. The way that the Spaniards do it is not like 'the good suit for a Sunday' syndrome that afflicted and still afflicts a minority of Scots, as it is more like 'the good suit, the good haircut, the good posture and the totally tremendous shirt and shoes'. They don't get dressed up to the nines, but to the tens, jacks, queens and kings, especially the queens, of which more later. In the later evening they parade around, displaying themselves, flirting if they are single, showing off the perfectly dressed and well-behaved offspring in wee suits and dresses, if they are married. Whole families, from great-grandfather on down move around in the warm and scented night air like groups of slow-moving, gossiping butterflies, pausing to sip nectar at any one of the dozens of brightly lit bars and cafés. It's a sight to see, and so were we.

There wasn't a dress kilt or a suit among us, though Billy had the full plaid kit, unwearable anywhere South of the Channel. 'It makes me sweat just looking at it in the wardrobe,' said Billy 'but I promised my daddy I'd wear it at the World Cup. It belonged to him. I'll wear it tonight.' And a doughty and brave warrior he looked, and was, as heatstroke was a distinct possibility.

Mahoney's kilt is a totally threadbare, ragged and faded Black Watch, worn without accoutrements. It belonged to his Uncle Tom, for whom he was named, as he was 'missing, believed killed' when Tom was born. His Uncle Tom was in fact captured with a bunch of Canadians with whom he was busy looting and fraternising his way up the Rhine when they got cut off by a counter attack. He spent nine months in a P.O.W. camp during which he wore his kilt continuously, having established, as welter-weight champion of his regiment, that anyone who made jokes about his kilt got their nose broken: right then. I know all this because I know Tam's Uncle Tom socially, and have heard him talk many times of how he ended up in the P.O.W. camp. At the time, Tam didn't know this, as he had been given the kilt as a family heirloom when he turned 21 and he was delighted, humble and determined, by turns. Auntie Mary got it off him and sewed a big tinsel thistle with ribbons in the colours of the Spanish flag into it in lieu of a sporran, and it looked really flash – something the people who voted him second in the contest realised, and also possibly because Tia and Tio had explained to hundreds of people the provenance of the kilt. But I'm getting ahead of the story.

'It's all about competitions,' said George 'so let's have one.' Big Andy said, 'Naw, three. Let's have three competitions. Best Dressed Scot, Best Dressed Spaniard and Best Dressed Russian.' Nobody so far had come up with a Russian, though Anne-Marie, Andy's future wife, knew all of their names and had pictures of the team. She volunteered to find and sponsor the best-dressed Russian. But she could not track one down. A couple of the guys had been to their base and the answer to everything was '*Nyet*'. This was pre-*Glasnost* and *Perestroika* was what Scotland could do with for the 1998 World Cup – a perr o strikers.

Billy had been for a look. 'They've got – you're not going to believe this – they've got big men in overcoats, unsmiling, nasty.'

George interjected 'So have the SFA,' but Billy wasn't to be deflected. 'They are every cliché in the book and an extra chapter on their own. If they are not KGB then I am my Auntie Jean's big yellow teapot.' We examined him for a spout, handle and colourisation and deduced that these men were indeed as reported. 'We could try a ploy on them,' suggested Sweeney, but Anne squashed this really bad idea with a glance. If there were any Russian supporters in Malaga they were keeping a very low profile indeed.

It was decided that a Russian fashion contest was out but Uncle Tio confounded us all by producing Alex, a man in at least his 70s who did the *paseo* with us for over an hour, dressed in the hammer and sickle, the Spanish flag, sandals and nothing else. Every now and then he would attempt a Cossack dance, encouraged by the Spanish clapping. He would manage three or four crouched steps and then fall on his arse, flashing his wares at all and sundry. The Kilt Police would have been proud of him. 'I've seen that thing so many times that it is beginning to interest me strangely,' said Anne-Marie to Anne, who tried to give her a reproving look but started to laugh, and they both ended up cackling like demented hens.

I think that Alex may have been a survivor of the Civil War, because all Uncle Tio's socialist and anarchist chums accompanied him round but we never did find out his story, as he collapsed from the drink and got carried off somewhere to recover. He won the Russian competition by acclamation and his prize was a litre bottle of vodka which Auntie Mary kept for him. The young Father was with us throughout handing out leaflets and being quite serious until someone mentioned masturbation, which happened quite a lot when he was around. He would then leave that table and join another, then the same thing would happen. He disapproved highly of Alex and of all Tio's chums. They weren't too keen on him either, but the enjoyment, the laughing and the San Miguel kept the peace, much aided by me, George and Mahoney. We kept an eye on them because if there was going to be any bother, they would be the source of it. They kept kind of growling at him and he would stare back.

The Spanish businessman we'd met in the Court had been with

us virtually all day and had drummed up a huge amount of interest in the contest. By this time there were hundreds of Scots moving from café to café with the Maryburgh Monster at the head, blowing his heart out. He hardly took any drink until the contest was over, seeing it as his patriotic duty, but when the winner was announced he drank about ten cubalibres in about ten minutes, was sick, and was placed sleeping in two chairs. He does this every night and it says something for our duty and his trust that we always make sure that he's okay.

But to the winners. The young Spanish guys were not too keen at first at showing themselves off, but they didn't mind flashing their girls around, and there were some stoaters. They got into it eventually, though, and were soon strutting up and down like catwalk veterans, stamping their feet and flashing their teeth. Big Andy suggested a sub-division of the contest, one for Least Dressed Female. The businessman announced this to the crowd to much approval, except from Anne, Auntie Mary and a few other women, as well as the priest, who told Sweeney that he was forbidden to encourage it. To be fair, the Spanish girls didn't seem all that keen, but Anne-Marie was. She'd had a few sherries and was positively itching to get her kit off. She's done it a couple of times since, but usually only when Andy is elsewhere, which is not a lot, as he disapproves highly of this – but only if it is Anne-Marie. That part of the contest was cancelled and as the short leet was drawn up, with Mahoney doing his mad celtic (and Celtic) warrior thing with a tray for a targe and a stick for a claymore, to much applause, a new entrant turned up. This entrant was Spanish, but very very dark, very Moorish, wearing a tiny kilt, a minuscule black bra with a lace shawl, and a mantilla, one of these lace crown things Spanish dancers wear, and high, square heeled dancing shoes. She was about six feet two inches, not counting the shoes, and she had a rose between her teeth. As she moved out into the space we'd cleared in front of the café, the crowd started to clap rhythmically, with us joining in inexpertly. What a dancer! As the clapping swelled and ebbed, faster and slower, she shimmied her hips, stamped her feet and clicked her fingers, uttering wee barking and whimpering noises by turn. The crowd knew her and shouts of 'Ay Carmel!' and ' A-r-r-r-r-iba!' were resounding in the square.

The priest, however, was an unhappy pixie, and this amused Tio and his chums greatly. They'd been a bit quiet as Carmel started ('Carmel!' said George, 'how sweet') but in the face of the priest's disapproval their encouragement increased. Anne leaned over and said something in John's ear making him look over at Carmel. He passed it on and it spread through the crowd. 'She's a guy,' said Mahoney in my ear, laughing like a drain, and soon you could see all the Scots trying to check for themselves as his/her kilt rose and fell. She loved the attention and danced faster and in a more focused fashion than ever, finally signalling her intention to finish to the crowd and, stopping with her arms up and her body impossibly elongated, rigid as an iron bar, she milked the applause of the crowd, eventually unbending and throwing her rose to Mahoney.

She was indeed a bloke, given name unknown, and she had brought her own supporters, as gay a bevy of hand flutterers as you could meet, clumped in a defensive wee bunch at a corner of the square, unsure of their reception, but bravely there, supporting their Dancing Queen.

Mahoney, rose between his teeth, bounded out into the space as the Monster's pipes wailed, and grabbed Carmel, swinging her into a wild improvised dance to 'Teeee-yeuch's!' from the Scots and 'Ay, ay, ay, ay, ay!' from the Spaniards.

As it came to an end, with the breathlessly laughing Carmel bowing and gesturing, Tam knelt in front of her and offered her the rose, bowing his head as she tapped him once with it on each shoulder.

It started at the corner where everyone was trying to make the gay group welcome, though I couldn't sing it for laughing and George nearly died from filling his lungs with gin and tonic. The famous Jimmy Hill anthem resounded around the square, but the 'we hate' was replaced by 'you'll love' and as it was explained to the Spanish people they started clapping rhythmically again and we all got up and danced. The Gay Gordons, obviously, had to be taught, and the images of these campy guys, some of them dancing with women, some with hulking tartan savages, remains fresh, and it is still one of the most talked about nights we've had. We were all going 'Na, na, na, na, na, na, nah' to the tune of *Scotland the*

Brave as we cavorted around, and a very fine time indeed was had by all. We even missed the Russian/New Zealand game, though some groups went and by the time the New Zealanders showed up George and I were helping each other home.

Next morning, discreetly drawing a veil over the odd incident that night, like Tio and his pals suggesting that crucifying the priest was Plan A, and making moves to do so, Sweeney and Mahoney were up and about at sparrowfart, organising backsliders, agnostics and why the fuck-nots along to Mass. I didn't go. Apparently I was woken and asked if I wanted to and declined politely, but I have no memory of this and neither does George, who was also asked.

This is Tam's version of events. He says, 'fucking' every three words, having been in the British Army, but I've left them out. Insert the word anywhere you like and you'll get close. 'Father Seb was chuffed. There were about 40 odd of us and he told us that there were lots more Spanish than usual. Some of the *Mariposas* were there as well, the first time they'd been.' ('*mariposa*' is Spanish for 'butterfly' but it also means 'gay', as does '*maricon*', a much harsher word.)

'So was Señor What's His Face, that guy in the suit. He was with a heavy religious team. Apparently he has a papal knighthood and is a big money raiser. Anyway, he was great and really friendly and Father Seb's sermon was about tolerance, he told me. Tio wasn't there, but Tia and a lot of other Spanish women were, and there was a real buzz about. The squad and any of the rest of the battalion are invited down to the *mariposas'* bar for free drinks, food, and a cabaret tonight.'

'We went, of course. The cabaret was totally outrageous – and that was just us. Anne-Marie did a strip, much to Andy's discomfort, and he, not to be outdone, got up on the tiny stage and sang a song titled "Wow" which I'm pretty sure he made up. The climax of the song came when Andy sang the last line "So I say . . ." and then he turned his back, flipped his kilt up and there on each buttock was a large "W" he then bent right over to spell out the word – but you've got the picture, and a pretty well received one it was, with everybody stamping and shouting "Wow!"'

Big Andy pronounces it 'Waw', said Sweeney. 'That's right,' said Mahoney to him, 'but if you'd looked really closely you would have seen a wee letter A from a Scrabble set stuck to his arsehole. It took me ages, that.' Sweeney nodded and looked at Tam a bit oddly saying 'I see, I see,' which he obviously hadn't, as Tam had just made it up on the spot.

Father Seb was there by request, though he only stayed for half an hour, arriving just in time for Andy's act. He was sitting between Mahoney and Sweeney and he opened his mouth to explain that Tam was lying but George caught his eye and then they both started laughing, the first time I'd seen Father Seb being anything less than serious. He was pressed up onto the stage and sang what I suspect was some kind of Latin religious song because the Spanish guys and maybe gals mostly crossed themselves when he had finished, and not a few had tears in their eyes. Before he left he went round shaking hands and leaving cards with his phone number, probably seeking converts and intent on extending the boundaries of the tolerance of his Church. He probably got a few calls, too, as he was an almost Gregory Peck lookalike, with big soulful eyes, and I'd noticed definite interest in him from more than a few of the people present, none of them female.

The biggest hit of the evening was Carmel, or MacCarmel as she now called herself, having been pronounced winner of both categories the previous night by virtue of being declared an honorary Scot. The last time I was in Malaga she owned a big bustling bar there called Carmels and I was welcomed with open arms (and open mouth, she kisses like a vacuum cleaner). She had organised an Abba group, the first time any of us had ever seen one, anticipating the wannabee and tribute bands by years. They were totally rotten, apart from the footwork. They didn't know the words to the songs and one of them kept burying his head in his hands and rushing giggling off the stage, but Carmel was superb, miming along to Dancing Queen and doing her own heavily accented Gimme, Gimme, Gimme (A Man After Midnight).

By the time the witching hour struck, the party was going strong, and the *mariposas* were intent on making conversions of their own. I don't know if they succeeded or not but I did hear one silk clad vision, on being rejected verbally somewhat robustly by Mahoney, saying to his friend 'But he is wearing a skirt!' I did not pass this along to Tam at the time, as he, along with the kilt, inherited his Uncle Tom's attitude to people who denigrate it in any way. There are gay members of the Tartan Army, but it is a pretty macho culture, and I've never met anyone who was upfront about it, at least not right away.

Anyway, by game time we had our own gay support group, as Carmel and four of her friends came with us. We marched up, with the Monster skirling along at the head of our clan, backs straight, carrying the hopes of a nation on our shoulders. We got in behind the huge banner that read 'Alcoholism versus Communism', but as Tio was with us as well, with some of his chums, it could have read 'Alcoholism and Communism'. There were tens of thousands of us, adrenalin dripping from the pores, slugging San Miguel to get rid of the taste of copper in our mouths. George grinned at me 'This is our World Cup Final, eh, Wee Man?' He was, as you know, as prophetic as ever, and we were to regret the two soft goals New Zealand put past us.

La Roselada, the stadium, was just like Hampden, tartan-wise, only around 40 degrees hotter. It must have been over 80 degrees in the stadium and if we were sweating just cheering and singing, imagine what it must have been like running about trying to beat the Russians, who had some really good players. We nearly did though, and if it hadn't been for Dasaev, a brilliant keeper, and Nicolae Rainea, an absolutely rotten referee, we would have. Rainea is from Rumania, still then under Ceaucescu, and he acted like he'd get shot if he even gave a foul against the Russians. We should have had at least two penalties, including one absolutely stonewall one late on when Wark was pulled down in the area. He also warned the Russians about time wasting and then as we were hammering furiously away at them after Souness scored the beaut with four minutes to go, he blew the whistle after playing only about ten seconds of extra time. The Steelman is a referee. He always brings his stopwatch to the games and he reckons we should have got another four minutes at least.

But that was it. Dreams in the dust again. Two each. Carmel and her friends were crying, their voices a lot rougher than they'd been, as they had spent the entire game shouting 'Es-co-ci-a, Es-

31

co-ci-a!' A wee boy of about eight or nine right in front of us was sobbing as if his heart would break, and more than a few of us were leaking copiously in the eye area. Not crying, you understand, just leaking copiously. Carmel and her pals were cuddling him, the made-up faces streaked with tears and mascara and the wee boy's dad looked like he was just about to join in.

We all stood with our arms around each other for a minute or two and as the wee boy's sobs subsided The Steelman gave him the shirt off his back. It was a Brazil strip, a trophy much prized by The Steelman, who had swapped with a Brazilian in one of the bars in Seville, and it was a major sacrifice on his part. The boy's dad was grateful. 'See you in Columbia,' he kept saying. 'We owe you one. See you in Columbia.' We didn't, of course, but we did see him, and his now strapping son, Jimmy, in Mexico, where a Brazil shirt was presented with due ceremony to The Steelman. I went and swapped my shirt later that night in Malaga and gave the Brazil shirt to The Steelman, which is why I don't have an '82 jersey, but he deserved it and it is up on the wall of his games room. He gave me the one he was presented with in Mexico, and it is on the wall in my room.

Outside the ground, the troops lined up for the long walk back into the square and the bus station. We had lost our dreams of glory, but we weren't defeated. Some of us had shed a lot of tears, and I for one was still doing so, but the heads were up. We'd played well and we'd gone out with honour. The Monster fired up his pipes and away we went singing 'We're No Awa' Tae Bide Awa' at the top of our voices.

The whole long way there were Spanish people clapping and cheering us, lining the streets, leaning out of the windows of their houses, standing up on tables in cafés to applaud, holding up wee bits of tartan or anything that resembled it, like checked table-cloths. I don't think that I've ever felt as proud to be Scottish as I was that night. It was just great.

When we got to the square there were thousands of people milling around saying their goodbyes, leaving on the bus and train for Torremolinos, Balmadena and the rest of the Costa del Sol, back to wives, weans and sanity, but the Tartan Army, like any other modern army has to be fast and adapt quickly to any situation, a fact which was demonstrated that night. We were all singing 'Cheerio, Cheerio, Cheerio', and the Spanish people were going '*Adios, Adios, Adios*'. The whole square was at it. There was a huge pole in the middle of the square and a former member of the Kilt Police had climbed almost to the top, past the fairy lights and the bunting it was supporting. As he conducted the '*Adios, Adios, Adios*', choir, he lost his grip and slid down the pole, his descent arrested when he hit the fairy lights, which promptly went out. Without missing a single beat the chant then became 'Burnt yer baws, burnt yer baws, burnt yer baws'. See flexible? See the Tartan Army?

And I finally, later that night at Tio's, got to learn all the words in Spanish to 'Long Live the Fifteenth Brigade', my favourite song of the Spanish Civil War.

4: Land of the Midnight Daughter

'Of course there's beer in Iceland' Shuggie sounds uncertain.

'There isny, there isny, the man's jist tellin me.' The Dummy, so called because he never ever shuts up, is hopping from foot to foot in his anxiety. The man, in this instance, is Uncle Ken Stewart, the SFA's security advisor. George and I approach him. 'That right, Ken?' says George. 'No beer in Iceland?'

'That's right.' Ken nods. 'No pubs either.'

Ripples are spreading round the airport departure lounge. 'No beer.' 'No whit?' 'Christ's sake.' People begin to walk towards the duty free, me among them. George is still talking to Ken but joins me as I'm halfway down the rapidly growing queue.

'You're allowed to take in 24 cans. You can get it at Keflavic Airport and take it into the country from there,' he says.

'I'll get a bottle of whisky here anyway on the grounds that if you can't buy beer they're likely to be funny about whisky. Do you want anything?' I ask.

'Some juniper juice,' he replies. I sigh inwardly. George and gin have got me into some carry-ons in the past.

Bodyswerve and Big Andy are just in front of me in the line.

'Listen Andy,' says Bodyswerve, 'I canny even carry wan day's worth of beer, never mind three.'

'Hard shite,' says Andy, who is six foot four, eighteen stone and among the world's worst losers at snooker. I once saw him overturn a full size table after losing a black ball game for 50 pence. Bodyswerve is about five foot five, eight stone and is called Bodyswerve because that is what everyone tries to do with him. He is an electrician and under sentence of death from Andy if he says 'us bright sparks' more than ten times a night. This figure has been negotiated downwards about five times since I've known him. Among other names for him mooted by the group are 'Two Short Planks', and 'The Brick'. But he's at every game and a good man in the crowd.

I poke Andy in the back. 'How's Anne-Marie and the weans?' I ask.

'Wee Man!' I am enfolded in his crushing bearhug. 'They're great, how's yours?' Amenities over, Andy is telling Bodyswerve and me who's here. 'Black Andy, Anne and Builder John, The Steelman, The Darkie.'

I pay for the whisky and gin and make my way to the bar, where I know I will find George and The Steelman. I am introduced to Hector, tiny, tartan clad from head to foot and on his first trip. He is bouncing up and down, grinning and chattering with infectious excitement.

Black Andy, a well-to-do coal merchant who once took Concorde to Madrid because the regular flight didn't give him time for a bevvy with the guys before the game, is doing one of his numbers on the barmaid.

'It's a drink. It's wee, brown and furry and it swims out to sea shouting "Fuck the Pope". Give up?' He crows. 'A bitter lemming – and put a gin in it.'

The P.A. tells us to start getting on the plane. We line up. Hector, George and Big Andy look like one of those 'The Development of Man', tableaux that you see in museums. Uncle Ken is lecturing the older guys. 'Keep an eye on the youngsters. Help them screw the bobbin. Give us a shout if it looks a real problem.'

We are all secretly proud of our reputation for good behaviour but this doesn't dampen the roar as we board.

Hector and Andy start to sing 'Here we go, here we go, here we go'. As they are cavorting down the aisle Andy picks Hector up and holds him out in front of him at head height and announces, 'The poison dwarves are here!'

We discover that we are sharing the plane with about two hundred sober businessmen from Boston, U.S.A. We later discover that they are sober because there is no drink on the plane. The shock on their faces was something to see, necks craned with blank 'Os' for mouths as they watched this tartan horde, carrying clinking bags, roaring at the tops of their voices, approach their sane existence. Communication was soon established when it transpired that we were prepared to share our carryouts even with Yanks. Fraternisation is difficult on a plane but ten minutes after take off there were Scots and Americans sitting together all over the plane. An American called Al was explaining the niceties of American football to George and me.

After about five minutes George, who has been caning the gin, says to him, 'That's no fitba, American fitba, yon Columbus was a fuckin dope.' He then proceeds to tell the story about what happened to all the shit Noah had to sweep off the Ark and concludes 'and it just lay there till Columbus discovered it.'

Al is a bit taken aback at George's vehemence, but I explain to him that George isn't anti-American, just pro gin and anti everything else, then I leave both of them to it.

The Steelman, a jeweller who lives in Leicester, is talking with another couple of Yanks, those innocent pale blue eyes, that have deceived dozens of gullible foreigners, blinking slowly. He catches my arm and introduces me as a geologist, 'PhD and Bar'. 'Tell my friends here about the Icelandic diamonds,' he demands.

I mutter something about volcanic cups, tectonic plates, flying saucers and lurch down to the bog, bumping into Uncle Ken in the queue. He tells me the Icelandic people are unhappy. It's illegal to drink on their planes, except for the wine with the meal. We discuss the fortune they could have made, pee, and get ready for landing.

Al and another American called Dave have been persuaded by George and the Steelman to come to the game, so they get off the plane with us. Instant chaos. Credit card waving. Smiling. Into the

Duty Free. I've never been in one going into a country before. We each pick up a box of 24 cans. Elephant lager. Piss. But we didn't know that then. Nor did we know that cans of beer were high value items in the black market in Reykjavik.

On the bus. It's about 50 kilometres to Reykjavik from the airport. From the windows to the horizon is desolation. Shades of grey, black and brown. Not a scrap of green anywhere as far as you can see. It looks worse than the moon. The light has a pearlised quality. Everything looks electrically charged. The Darkie says, 'I spy with my little eye, something beginning with L,' and about half the bus yells 'Lava!' This becomes a running joke for the rest of the trip. BL is brown lava. GL grey lava etc., etc.

Al and Dave are asking about The Darkie. He used to be called Alan Glen until late one night, after he had proclaimed belligerently several times that he would 'rather be a Darkie than a Tim', he looked up to find every finger in the pub levelled at him and Builder John intoning, 'Henceforth, you are The Darkie'. Non-sectarianism is a bit of a religion with most of us.

Explaining Scottish religious bigotry to two Bostonians only took George a minute, and as Anne shouted, 'A building, a building!' we all crowded to the side of the bus to see the aluminium smelting plant. There is a major shortage of scenery until we arrive in Reykjavik, which is full of brightly painted houses made of wood and corrugated iron and looks about the size of Hamilton.

The team were just leaving for the match as we rolled up to the hotel. 'Good luck, boys. All the best.' The team look tense but glad to see us and as they file on to their own bus Billy the Actor yells 'Break a leg, Graeme!' Souness looks up and smiles like a shark. 'Thanks. I'll try.'

Billy, who really is an actor, is explaining to Al and Dave about not wishing people in the theatre good luck because it's bad luck so you say 'Break a leg' or something similar. 'Do you think Souness knows that?' asks George. Quick change act at the hotel. Into the jerseys and onto the bus for the game.

When we arrive at the ground I discover, shock horror, that I have left the ticket in my jacket. Struggling against the tide of Icelanders I finally get a taxi to the hotel and back with the driver going like the clappers and blasting the horn continually. These people are the most aggressive drivers I have ever seen. Paris, New York, Rome – I've seen them and these people are a lot worse. He drops me a few hundred yards from the ground and I ceremonially hand him what's left of my half litre of Glenfiddich along with the fare. Uncle Ken has got us well trained. Two young Icelanders share their bottle with me as we walk to the gate. It is a local brew called Brennivin – these guys call it Black Death – and it certainly tastes lethal.

At the game, once the sky divers, the strongest man in the world, and the dancers were out of the way, out trooped a 40-strong choir – with a grand piano. They sang the Icelandic National Anthem and then *Scotland the Brave* – every word of every verse – with all the Scots in the crowd going 'Na, na, na, na, na, na, na,' with red faces.

Scotland started the game well and were on top until Souness caught one of their better players an absolute sickener, putting him out of the game and causing the Icelandic bench to erupt. Their English manager is screaming 'Bastard' at Souness and one of their subs tries to attack Stein. The team lost its rhythm at that point but after Leighton's penalty save I said to Builder John, 'We'll win this one. We'll get a lucky goal with five minutes to go.' 'You're on your dinner if we do,' says Anne.

Big Andy thumps down beside me. 'I was just talking to Rod Stewart in the bog,' he says.

'Oh aye, what did he say?' I ask.'He said, "You're pissing on my shoes, mate!"'

The game has settled down into a lacklustre shuffling from end to end with one goal definitely going to be the winner. When Bett finally cracked it in the release of tension was enormous. Amid the celebrations Al and Dave are chanting 'Scotland! Scotland! Zizz, Boom, Bah! Scotland! Scotland! Ra, Ra, Ra!'

They have not got the slightest idea what is going on on the field but they are having a great time. They are also falling down a lot and feeling no pain whatsover, having drunk a litre bottle of 'Scatch' between them since we landed.

Game over. One nil to us. We're a bit deflated. We didn't play well and didn't really deserve to win. We shake hands with the

Icelandic fans and invite a few back to the hotel. 'Ah, where the girls are, yes,' says one of them, whose name, I discover, is Halldor Halldorson.

On the bus back to the hotel Big Andy, who is called Big by the Icelanders, says, 'I want you to meet a man who fought a volcano to a draw.' This guy is called Jonaton and he tells us the story of Heimaey, his home, which I vaguely remember from the television news. It was engulfed by pumice and threatened by lava but they fought it with seawater for five months, finally cooled it and dug their town out again. A determined and brave people.

George and The Steelman are by now carrying the Americans, and we dump them in George's room. They are now part of the Room Committee, as the hotel was full when we arrived. The Room Committee consists of people who have no rooms. That is, they don't belong in the hotel. It may be guys who aren't working or just can't afford it but who have made it to the game anyway by hitching or whatever, so the ones with rooms put them up on their floors. Usually there are a lot but Iceland is a difficult place to get to so there are only a dozen or so. I often wonder if the hotel managers in the ones that have big Room Committees think we all eat three breakfasts each, because breakfast is usually free, so everybody stocks up for the day.

We go up to the tiny bar before dinner but we can't get near it as it is filled with women and girls, some of whom are absolutely stunning.

'Is there a beauty contest?' asks The Steelman.

'Naw, the bus crashed on the way here and we are actually in Paradise,' says George.

As we threaded our way to the bar I was fondled at least twice and caught one unmistakeable wink. Carrying our drink-laden trays we edged our way over to the group, now about ten strong. 'What are all these women doing here?' asks Anne of Halldor. The Icelandic guys look a bit uneasy. 'They are here for you, for the Scots. It is a thing of our culture. It is called, I believe, exogenesis – marrying outside the tribe.' Halldor goes on to explain that illegitimacy is perfectly normal in Iceland and that women are as free sexually as men.

'Marrying, aye, that will be right!' snorts Anne as she grasps

Builder John and me firmly by the elbows and marches us to the restaurant.

As John is buying I opt for caviar for the first course – which is delicious and only £2.00. The waiter recomended the special Icelandic smoked lamb at £3.50 which we all order.

'Local food is always cheaper,' says Anne when I express pleased surprise at the quality and price. I had been told that Iceland was expensive. The entire meal was wonderful and John worked out that the bill would be £21.00. It was £210.00. 'These decimal points are dodgy wee bastards.' sighs John. Anne is in shock. '£35.00 for a bit of lamb!' I point out that there are dearer things on the menu and with our newly acquired decimal expertise we plan a meal for three which only costs £340.00, not counting wine. John refuses to divulge what the wine cost but I finally prevail on them to split the bill. God bless credit cards.

We are joined by Big Andy, The Steelman and Hector, each accompanied by an Icelandic lady. 'Holmfridur here,' says Andy 'says she wants to have a baby with me because I'm strong and laugh all the time.' There is awe in his voice. Hector introduces Valgerdur who is at least 20 years older than him. 'She says I remind her of her grandfather.'

On the way to the toilet I turn a corner and bump into a couple writhing against the wall. The guy, whom I don't know, is about 18 and she is about 16. 'I'm with the Room Committee,' he says, looking at me with pleading eyes. The girl is unbelievably beautiful. I give him my key, instructing him to leave it at the desk.

Back in the bar Valgerdur is explaining their names. Is is illegal in Iceland to call your child by a non-Icelandic name, and everybody is called by their mother or father's Christian name with 'son' or 'dottir' added. 'So all of the women in the bar are called something dottir?' asks George. 'This is the land of the midnight daughter.'

It is by this time past midnight, though that oddly phosphorescent light is still everywhere as I make my way to the front desk. No key.

Couples are everywhere.

I had a quick go at a bounce game in the corridor, during which Hector and his lady gave a good account of themselves, and

Hector earned the name 'Hector Toetector', for his cavalier attitude to other peoples' shins.

I knock softly at my room door, feeling like a brothel keeper, and shout, 'Five minutes,' but the door opens immediately and the girl, clad only in panties, grins cheekily at me and says 'You come to join us?' The guy, who introduces himself as John Maguire, is just finishing putting clean sheets on the bed. Considerate kids, if a trifle smug.

After they'd gone, with John saying 'That's one I owe you, Wee Man,' I fell asleep instantly, fully clothed, to be woken at 4 a.m. by the Americans, now fully recovered, demanding Action.

It is still light outside, the corridors are still busy. Armed with George's gin we find a room party, at which I instantaneously fall asleep, to awaken in my own bed, still fully clothed. By all accounts I missed an orgy.

After breakfast, a bunch of us went on a nine hour tour of Iceland. Saw glaciers, volcanoes, giant waterfalls, the original Geysir, after which all others are named, Strokkur, which had the good grace to erupt while we were there. I stood with my feet astride a fissure that becomes two different continents. Big Andy comments that the whole country is cracked and when told that these continental masses are moving apart at eight millimetres per year asks the guide what they fell out over. 'It couldny have been very serious.'

The Steelman, who has formed the biggest lava collection in private hands in Europe, is ejected from the bus for his latest 'I spy' which is 'Gigantic great galumphing gobs of green goo' – a reference to the moss which occasionally colours the lavascape. When we went back to get him five minutes later he had hidden himself among the lava and it took us 15 increasingly frantic minutes to find him.

Just before we got back to Reykjavik, Valgerdur translates a bit of the local paper the gist of which is 'We look forward to a crop of Scottish babies in nine months time.'

'It's in the paper!' Bodyswerve is thunderstruck.

'Ahm movin' here,' he says.

'Aye, but then you'll not be a stranger,' says The Steelman. Bodyswerve ponders this dilemma and the next day, on the plane home, bursts out 'Ah could visit!'

After we had eaten we all trooped up to the TV lounge for the European Cup final, to find Anne and John, grey faced, sitting watching the atrocity that was Heysel unfold. Their oldest son, Ian, the only Liverpool supporter in Inverness, is at the game. Anne keeps shouting 'I see him, there he is' as the camera pans across the bodies. Ian, sensible guy that he is, left the game and phoned home knowing they would be frantic. His brother phoned the hotel and reassured them. After about 20 more minutes of mindlessness from the fans and ineptitude from the Belgian police, the Icelandic TV station pulled the plug, leaving us staring at a blank screen.

'There but for the grace of God,' says George, voicing the thoughts of everyone in the room.

5: Bodyswerve's Baby

Bodyswerve just can't leave things alone. He goes on and on and on – some of the group still call him Ariston from that old TV advert – until someone, usually Big Andy, who is more than twice his weight, growls at him to shut up. Usually he does, but the Icelandic trip was a bit different. He would not shut up about this woman who had picked him up. As I explained in the previous story, the women in Iceland, apart from mostly being very good looking, tend to pick their men, rather than the other way round, and a lot of the group found this quite difficult to handle.

Billy the Actor and I were carrying George, who was already juniper-juiced out of his brain before he ordered what they call 'beer' in Iceland. What they give you is a bottle of non-alcoholic beer, which tastes like a very thin dilution of Fairy Liquid, and then they put a shot of pure grain alcohol in it. 'Your horse, sir, has a very bad case of diabetes,' said George, to the club owner, after cautiously sipping his first one, but it didn't stop him drinking another two or three before shouting 'In fact, sir, I would have it put down' and then crashing full-length across two booze-laden tables.

By the time we had bought new drinks for the somewhat miffed and fairly tough-looking Icelanders, George was out about £30 and like a light. He was comatose, totally zonked. Billy and I got him out of the door all right but we were having a bit of a job carrying him.

As we dragged him round the corner, to return to the tale, we met two lads from Perth that we'd seen with the women in the hotel bar earlier. 'Ye didnae get a click, then?' asked Billy, who is from Aberdeen and really does talk like the *Sunday Post* sometimes. 'Naw. They kept asking us but bawface here couldn't handle it.' The speaker is called Jake, often called Jake the Sheik or Jake the Trouser Snake, because he is a skirt-chaser without peer. This is a guy who turned up at a wedding in Cyprus with what he called 'a genuine certified virgin'. She looked about 13 and he's well into his 30s. The Greek Cypriots who had invited us (once we'd gatecrashed) weren't over the moon with this description of her but he kept asking them 'Where's your virgin, then?' until one of them had to be held back by his mates. Jake is competitive, unscrupulous and loves games and ploys, so maybe he was winding them up, but none of us think so. I haven't seen the pal he called bawface since but I suspect that it was Jake's manhood that was challenged in Iceland.

The two of them had just bought fish suppers, delicious cod with weird tasting chips, and they were a bit bemused by the fact that they had cost £18 each. Billy told them that the cod was free and it was the potatoes that cost all the money. They nodded as if Billy knew what he was talking about and when they'd finished their platinum fish suppers they gave us a hand back to the hotel with George.

As we came out after having put George in the recovery position i.e. flung on top of his bed with his shoes off, there was Bodyswerve with a quite pleasant looking woman. 'We've done it twice already,' was his greeting. None of the 'How's it going, have a beer,' nonsense for this shooter of fish in barrels. We found out much, much later that he'd never been with another woman since he was married, but I'm getting a bit ahead of myself.

Bodyswerve was in his pomp. There was something quite endearing about his glee and his childish pride, but over the next couple of days we heard every detail of what he and his lady had done, every moan, sigh and sexual position. None of us wanted to know, but he wouldn't stop talking about it. He even spoke of moving to Iceland until George pointed out that that would place Bodyswerve's wife in the same position as the other women in Iceland. That shut him up for a while but soon he was back at 'and then she said "touch me here" and I went . . .' and so on. The only solution was to fill him full of drink or to talk about football, about which he is immensely knowledgeable.

We did this at every opportunity until we flew home, not to Glasgow but to Prestwick in the middle of the night, which is a whole other story about money and a stupid disagreement between the airline and Glasgow airport, which inconveniences hundreds of passengers. Hector got quite incensed when he heard this and hid bits of cod all over the plane. He had taken fish to Iceland, his own personal apology for the Cod War, and was mildly famous for this among the fishermen at a club we'd been to. They'd given him some of their fish straight out of the sea that morning but I imagine that some of it was quite a bit older before it was found, as it was stuffed into every nook and cranny that he could find.

We thought we had heard the last of Bodyswerve and his Icelandic non-maiden, but we hadn't. About ten or 12 weeks after we got back, Scotball forwarded a letter to him which was addressed to him at Park Gardens. They sent it to his home and he nearly died when he opened it. It was from Astrid and she wrote of her joy at her possible impending motherhood and of how happy and proud she would be if the sprog was anything like him. There was also some fairly juicy stuff about what they had done and what she would like to do next time they met. Bodyswerve was on the phone to Big Andy, who lives near him, about half an hour after he got it, totally panic stricken, because she was talking also of coming to visit him in Dunfermline, where, apparently unbeknownst to Astrid, he already has a wife. Andy got him round to the pub and helped him write a letter to Iceland. Bodyswerve doesn't read or write all that well and Andy is not the most articulate of men. This is the text of the letter in full.

Dear Astrid,
Thank you very much for your letter and for the good

news. I think that I maybe have to go to Saudi Arabia in
2 or 3 days to work but I'll write to you from there, if I
have to go which I think I might have to. I'm pleased
that you're pleased about the baby. I hope it has your
eyes.
Love
From John.

They put Andy's home address on it and about two weeks later
another letter arrived on Andy's mat. This was about five pages
long, confirming that yes, she was expecting a baby and had he
gone to Saudi, and she was looking forward to seeing him if and
when he came to Iceland. There was more juicy stuff as well and
she said that compared to Icelandic men he was a giant. He's
about five foot five and skinny, with, as Andy says 'less fat on him
than a chip', but Astrid had obviously met her prince and she was
seeing him through romantic eyes. At least that's what Bodyswerve
thought. George and I and half a dozen of the other guys knew
different. George, a man who regards marital infidelity with the
same kind of fastidious distaste as he does the tabloid football
press, had stormed out of the hotel bar one night in a fury at
Bodyswerve and had decided to teach him a lesson.

A few of us had met the British Consul after the game in Iceland
and George enlisted his help. All of the letters that Bodyswerve
received were in fact written by George and, with the Consul's
help, posted from Iceland. George is a professor of English, with
the entire canon of romantic prose and poetry in his repertoire,
and he had gone to town. The half dozen or so letters that he
wrote are minor masterpieces of erotic fiction. Andy was doing his
best to reply in kind, and of course passing the results straight to
George via his company's fax, but the contrast was very evident.
George/Astrid would be full of things like 'How do I love thee?
Let me count the ways' and some talk of 'star-crossed lovers' and
'two souls with but a single thought' while Bodyswerve/Andy's
would say 'I remember your hair. It was a very nice shade of
brown.'

The second last one that George wrote spoke of her lusting after
his body and how pregnancy was changing her body and making

her randy all the time. It was the second-last one because after he received it Bodyswerve did something that he hadn't done before and of which none of us had thought him capable. He wrote a letter to Astrid himself, without consulting Andy, and sent it to the address on the letter. George of course had ensured that it was the address of the British Consulate, in case Andy had had to actually post a letter while Bodyswerve was there, so he had it faxed through to the Uni.

He then phoned me for a consultation because the letter put a slightly different complexion on things. I haven't actually seen that one but it said something like, 'Dear Astrid, I am married but I want to talk to you about something important.' Andy was given the delicate job of finding out what it was that was important without letting on that he knew about the letter, but Bodyswerve, proud as punch, started telling Andy all about how he'd written his own letter and that he had made a decision to support the child financially. He was also trying to get up the courage to talk to his wife about Astrid and the baby. This was getting into deep water for Andy so he told Bodyswerve that the best thing to do was not to discuss it with his wife before he had heard back from Astrid and then rushed round to convey this to George.

George then decided to put an end to the ploy before it got any further out of hand and he sat down and wrote a bitter and hurt letter full of wounding words like 'betrayal' and 'the death of all my hopes', and saying that she didn't want his baby now that she'd discovered what a rat he was. The letter also said that she was coming to Glasgow to shop for maternity and baby clothes and that he could meet her at the airport. It also went on at some length about the cost of keeping a baby and asked just how responsible did he feel.

The plan was then that all of the Icelandic mob who could make it would be at the airport at the specified time, conceal ourselves and then jump out on Bodyswerve if he turned up. Big Andy advised us that he had indeed decided to go and that he seemed quite chuffed at the thought of seeing her again. Andy had only talked to him on the phone and he was a bit miffed that Bodyswerve hadn't asked him to come with him, for immoral support or whatever. 'Maybe he's ashamed,' he said, 'but I thought that he would ask me. He's sounding a bit funny.'

On the appointed day the merry pranksters, me and George included, met in the Horseshoe Bar. Counting Jim from Perth was there with his brand new video camera and we were altogether a jolly bunch. We had lunch and a couple of beers while the non-Glaswegians marvelled at being charged only £1.50 for three courses of good plain food. George, not a Glasgow man or a Glasgow fan, said of the mince that Counting Jim had just had, 'that was probably an Edinburgh man you just ate, that's why it's so cheap', and Big Andy the Fifer said 'Aye, I thought it tasted a bit queer'.

Then it was off to the airport for the fun and games. We changed into the strips and scarves in the toilets at the airport and went up and hid in the bar, positioning a couple of lookouts to keep us posted of Bodyswerve's arrival. We got some odd looks as we walked through the airport and a very nattily suited businessman asked if we were an advance or a rear guard of the Tartan Army. We were puzzled at people looking at their wrists as we went past until George realised that they were checking the date, thinking they'd missed out on news of a game.

Jim came pelting into the bar, having left someone else videoing the arrival, saying 'He's here. He's just going to the arrivals board'.

The plane was on time and we sneaked down the stairs. The idea was to get as near as we could to the arrivals lounge but to keep out of Bodyswerve's sight until all the passengers had gone through, then to rush him. He spoiled this plan by noticing Andy, who is about as inconspicuous in his Scotland kit as a double-decker bus. The passengers were starting to come through as he shouted 'Andy' and waved him over. Then he saw me and George, so we strolled over trying to look casual. He had on a good suit and he was carrying a huge bunch of flowers. Just as George and I arrived, with Counting Jim videoing the encounter, Andy's face suddenly went rock solid in shock. Bodyswerve was rabbiting away 'What brings you here? How's it going? What's the gear on for?' when he noticed the woman that Andy had just seen approaching from the direction of the Ladies. 'This is the wife,' said Bodyswerve. 'Margaret, these are some of my Tartan Army mates.'

The word 'wife' hung in the air, quivering with future pain. 'Oh fuck,' mouthed George, as the rest of the guys strolled up. Bodyswerve was still prattling away but he noticed that we'd all gone a bit quiet. His wife was looking at us and she knew something was wrong.

The last of the Icelandic passengers was gone and George stepped forward and said 'It was a ploy, John. I'm sorry.' John didn't understand. 'What ploy, who's it on?' He was still looking around for Astrid. When the penny dropped, the blood drained from his face and his knees sagged. His wife grasped his arm and threw the flowers at George. Her face was flaming. Her private humiliation was public. She'd been twice betrayed, once by him and once by us. She dragged him out of the building without a word, though if looks could kill, and hers were the closest to it I've ever experienced, then we would all be grease spots on the airport parquet.

That was bad enough, but we got the full spec from Andy the next day, and it was worse. The marriage was already under strain because they were mutually infertile. They'd been trying to have a child for a long time with no success, and when Bodyswerve told her about Astrid he'd already worked out the plan that they'd adopt the child if they could. You can imagine the kind of torture that she must have put herself through, and the desperation that made her agree to come with him to meet this woman, who was having her husband's baby. Then to discover that it was a joke perpetrated by blue-clad clowns who had no idea.

We filtered away, feeling very stupid. George said '*Mea Maxima Culpa*' and said that he would send a hugely apologetic letter, which he did, with all our names, saying that if there was ever, ever anything at all that we could do to make up for our crassness, then she just had to ask.

She hasn't yet, and the story has got a kind of a happy ending. They split up and both are now remarried with one child each, born in the same hospital about three weeks apart. She and Bodyswerve are still talking to each other but she isn't talking to us at all. He is, though, and he has never embarked on another romantic adventure of any kind. 'No worth it,' he says, when asked to admire some foreign lady by one of the lads, and he's right.

6: The Flower of Scotland

As long as he lived, he was the guiding star of a whole brave nation and when he died the little children cried in the streets.

MOTLEY *The Rise of the Dutch Republic*

'He's died. He's dead. Ah heard it on the radio.' Bodyswerve's face is a strained mask. 'I wish we hudny come. I wish ah wis at hame.' He starts to cry, struggling hard to hold back the tears in front of his mates.

'It's Jock,' Big Andy confirms. 'A heart attack.'

George and I had been behind the dugout and had seen him collapse shortly after the penalty and get carried inside. We'd seen Fergie's face just after the whistle, when he sent the team back out to applaud the crowd, and we knew something was wrong, but we had not yet confronted tragedy.

It had taken us nearly 20 minutes to reach the pub through packed crowds of jubilant Scottish fans emulating John Rambo. 'Don't push me! Don't push me.' After 20 repetitions of this George says 'I preferred Rimbaud when he was a French poet.'

The two Welshmen the Steelman brought to the game with him, both called Ivor, one instantly dubbed 'The Engine' the other 'Big Yin', helped us through the stiff bodies, the hostile hard eyes, the finely controlled black rage, when we got to the Welsh supporters. We had just robbed them of their trip to Mexico with yet another soft penalty. Their restraint was admirable. The Steelman was at his best. 'Nae Luck! Still a chance though! You were unlucky. See you in Mexico!' Shaking hands with people whose dreams of glory had been destroyed by a fluke, who had beaten us on our own ground, the Steelman starts, 'If you hate the fucking English clap your hands.' We all join in. The storm of clapping that follows reaffirms the Celtic bond. A small dark, square built man is pumping my hand. 'The enemy of my enemy is my friend. Where are you going?'

By the time we get to the pub, our ranks have been swelled by a dozen Welshmen from this encounter.

As the news sank in and the solemn-faced television announcer confirmed it, our national groups draw apart.

Big Andy started our wake, tears pouring from his eyes and dripping from his beard, he stands foursquare in his kilt, big fist hammering the bar, 'who fought and DIED for!'

Bodyswerve and I are struggling with Mahoney, who just wants to damage somebody. He is hurting both of us. Bodyswerve's nose is bleeding. George and Builder John grab Mahoney from behind. Anne says to him 'Terrific, Tam, Jock would have loved that!' provoking a storm of weeping from Mahoney. Later he explained that he was crying for Jock, and his own father who had died four months before. 'Ah couldny cry before, Wee Man. I'm sorry if I hurt you. I'll get everybody a drink.'

The two groups in the bar were still apart and there was a sense of gloom, of shared grief hovering over both. The Steelman's pal, Ivor the Engine, comes over and asks us to join the Welsh group. People are talking quietly. A little Welsh lady in her 50s says it reminds her of Aberfan. Bodyswerve says 'Aberfan, was that here? Oh Christ, I'm awful sorry missus!' He hugs her and she dissolves in tears, telling us of her sister's child, who died there.

George stands up, smoothing out a crumpled piece of paper. 'I'm going to make a wee toast.

'Jock Stein was my hero, and a man respected and admired beyond his nationality and skills as a football manager. He carried a sense of self respect, of fairness and decency, with him like an aura. He loved football and football loved him. He was a working-class hero who never forgot his roots, the father, brother or uncle we could all be doing with. I loved him because he helped create the strength and pride in ourselves and our country which will enable us to go on without him. We are bereft, but I know his spirit lives on in all of us. Ladies and Gentlemen, Mr Stein!'

A Welshman silently toasted, drained his glass and smashed it in the fireplace, but George said 'None of that, he's worth more than broken glasses, give us a song.'

We all joined in when they started singing 'Bread of Heaven', then the Welsh sang 'Cwym Rhondda'. I couldn't understand a word, but it raised hairs on the back of my neck.

Andy sang 'The Land of the Leal' and one of the Welsh bassists recited a poem. It ended up as a kind of chant and he did it twice. It has three verses each of which starts and ends with 'And Death Shall Have No Dominion' and contains the lines, 'Where blew a flower may a flower no more, lift its head to the blows of the rain,' which started us all off on 'Flower of Scotland' again.

Several of the guys who were staying out of town had been asked home by people in the bar. Here were these people whom I'd always thought of as bitter and intense, opening their homes and their hearts. One of the Ivors was explaining to someone who hadn't been at the game that Neville Southall was probably one of the last people to shake Jock Stein's hand. 'Before the start all the practice balls had been kicked past him into the crowd at the Scots end and they kept them, like, to upset Neville. But Stein noticed this, went down to that end and made the crowd give the balls back. Then he shook Neville's hand and it looked as if he was wishing him luck. A measure of the man.'

Suddenly, everyone is telling everyone else their Stein stories. Bobby Mac from Motherwell found more than £100 left over from the Iceland trip in his blazer and slapped it on the bar. Rohbat and Darryl, the guy who smashed his glass in tribute to Jock, asked the bar owner to stay open a while and he agreed. There was talk of heroes and funerals. We talked of the shock to his family of finding out from the telly or the radio. 'Ernie Walker will have phoned them,' says Anne, 'he's that kind of man.' We all knew she was right. Darryl is saying to a couple of other Welsh people, 'They gave Neil [Kinnock] a big round of applause, did the Scots. They did him proud.'

'But did you see them at the penalty? Not a bloody one was looking! They were all bloody praying.'

'We'll all be praying tonight for something, son,' says Builder John to the Welshman 'and it will be a lot more important than that. I'd give up 20 World Cups to still have Jock with us.'

There are murmurs of agreement and we started to filter outside. The streets were quiet, with wee knots of people quietly talking. In the hotel bar we sang a few sad songs and went to bed.

We didn't see the wreath at the ground the next day, but we saw the television pictures. The man or woman who laid it spoke for all of us.

'Jock. Heroes live for ever!'

7: The Hitchhiker's Guide to Seville Airport

'What time? *Que ora?* Shit'. Seville 8.40 a.m. and my plane leaves at 8.45 a.m. I prise open my eyes, ignoring the San Miguel-induced blinding pain, and try to take stock. Yes, I'm in my own hotel room. That's one big plus. Yes, the nice Spanish lady on the phone was right except that it is now 8.43 a.m. on my watch. That's a major minus. Scotland got beat one-nil last night and if I miss this plane the lovely Marjory will kill me. Another two minuses. Decision time. Blissful slumber – the coward's way – postpone all thought and let the day take care of itself, or the grown-up way, feet out of bed, hangover-racked body forced into action, people to be dealt with, facts to be faced. Decisions, decisions.

Seventeen minutes later a rough hand is shaking me awake once again. 'Wee Man, Wee Man, you've missed your plane.' The rough hand, and we're talking badger's arse here, belongs to Peter, AKA Storchy the Battery Boy for reasons too complicated to go into without an hour to spare. Peter is one of the Room Committee and as I raise my head I can see three or four more. Memory seeps back. The game. The feeling of the inevitability of defeat when we'd been told Kenny couldn't play. The impulse to get blind drunk afterwards. The meeting with the roomless Room Committee. The umpty zillion drinks charged against my room number by said Room Committee. Peter is still shaking me. 'The plane might be late, go to the airport.' He's right. I'll phone. Nice Spanish lady phones me back two minutes later. Plane gone.

Bye-bye plane, hello deep shit. I have already incurred the displeasure of the lovely Marjory from the SFA for missing the bus back from the Under-21 game in Cadiz the night before last and my wife made me swear before I left that I'd be home for my daughter's big night on stage in the school play. Action time. Legs out of bed. Feet do not strike cold hard floor but instead warm yielding shouting substance that turns out to be the lower stomach and testicles of yet another of the Room Committee. Apologise. Into shower. Hastily collect gear and stuff into bag. Peter hands me a bundle of banknotes. 'I collected it from the guys. You might need it for the plane. It was our fault you slept in.' As at least three of the guys are still sleeping the sleep of the dead, assuming that the dead twitch, mutter and fart loudly, I imagine that there might be some recriminations when they wake up and find their money gone, but I take it anyway.

In the taxi to the airport I gradually wake up. The driver is a Real Betis supporter who thinks Spain will win the World Cup. They struggled to beat us by one goal so I doubt it but not out loud. I did that night before last in Cadiz and nearly got lynched by a bunch of Pepe's friends in the café. Pepe was why I missed the bus, but that's another story.

When we got to the airport I went to the desk and asked about my plane, pretending that I thought it left in half an hour. The oldish woman explains in slow, simple Spanish that I am eff you kay tee.

My plane is gone, vamoosed, vanished into the calm blue yonder. I asked her about other planes, thinking plane to Madrid, Madrid–London, London–Glasgow but she explains that it is a religious holiday and every plane going anywhere is completely, totally and utterly stuffed with Spaniards going to see their families. This woman is a fair hand with the adjectives but her moustache is beginning to develop a Zapata-like sneering cast and

I finally recognise a trait in her, widespread in Scots women of this age also. Self righteousness. She knows I am a drunken bum who slept in and she is really quite glad that I am feeling awful. I asked her if Spanish waiters all grow moustaches so that they will look like their mothers and stumbled off to the bar. On the way there I am intercepted by *Los Gigantes* – a bunch of Aberdeen supporters who are all at least six feet three inches tall. They got their nickname last night in one of the bars we were in. Manolo, the big daft Spanish guy with the drum and the flat shiny hat, named them. Manolo gets a grant from the Spanish government to support Spain, he told me. Funny old game, football.

'What's the matter, Wee Man, you look as if you've lost a pound and found a tanner,' says one of them. I explain. 'Well you'll just come on our plane then,' says Flembo, who is about the biggest of them. 'We'll get you home.' Flembo is all excitement. 'A ploy, a fair ploy,' he keeps saying. What the hell, I think. We can only get caught and then I'll have a real excuse for not getting home.

In for a peseta, in for a pound. Their plane is due to leave in about half an hour and has just been called. After a lot of discussion about disguising me as a sack of onions or a giant carry-out, sane opinion i.e. mine, prevails. I will walk aboard with them surrounding me and we will do a fun fantasy and confusion number on the stewardesses.

Getting aboard was an absolute doddle. I even got a boarding card in the shuffle. I still have it. But the next 20 minutes were difficult. They counted us. Then they counted us again. Then they counted us one more time. In the meantime Flembo and Mackie had tucked a 12-year-old Dundee United supporter called David into one of the overhead luggage dookits. When the stewardess opened it he shouted 'Boo!' and she nearly died. She was obviously expecting a terrorist attack. By this time everyone on the plane except the cabin crew knew who the illegal passenger was but nobody was cracking a light. Everybody kept shooting wee glee-filled glances anywhere but at me. Eventually, the façade of authority maintained by the airline people cracked and after counting us eight or nine times the captain announced that he knew that we knew that we had a stowaway and could he (or she – hastly added as an afterthought) please identify himself. Silence.

Broken by Flembo who is by now sitting on the folddown seat used by the stewardesses. 'You just sit on my knee, quine, and we'll hope for a bumpy take off.' Patsy, the red haired stewardess addressed by Flembo, suddenly starts to laugh loudly and, all flustered, bustles up the aisle to talk to the captain.

The intercom then said 'Okay, you win. We're taking off in two minutes.'

Muffled cheer. Patsy returns, and without even the glimmer of a smile, sits on Flembo's knee and buckles them both in.

As the plane is hurtling along the runway a soberly suited guy in his 60s reached across the aisle and took my hand. He smiled at me and said, 'You seem like a lucky bastard, and even if we do crash I'll die holding the hand of a Scotsman.' He is trembling like the San Andreas fault on piecework.

'If not to heaven then hand in hand to hell,' says a guy behind us. '*Richard the Third*' says the guy holding my hand. Erudite lot, these North Easters, even if they are scared of flying.

Once off the ground he let go of my hand, summoned the stewardess and filled one of the plastic glasses she brought with brandy from his duty free. Patsy told him that it was illegal to drink your own booze on the plane and he says 'But it's okay to pick up hitchhikers?'

After I'd drunk the brandy the headache went away but things started to get blurry. One minute I was involved in a group rendering such classics as 'Ay, ay, ay, ay! Tiswas is better than Swapshop' and the next I was on the flight deck, nodding soberly while the captain explained about trim and throttling back and stuff like that.

I went to sleep for half an hour and when I woke up the plane had run out of beer. Flembo and his pal Doughnut are loudly demanding that we stop somewhere for more. There is a feeling abroad that we are running this plane.

Duncan, he of the hand-holding, is beginning to look worried again. He says 'Na, na, were safe enough here. Let's stay up.' Flembo, Duncan and I arranged a pooling of the carry-outs and they lasted well, though I don't recommend crème de menthe with tonic, even if the Pope does drink it.

I was back in my seat, planning how to get back to Glasgow

from Aberdeen when the view of the ground suddenly became familiar. 'The Clyde, that's the Clyde.' I said to Duncan. 'Aye, we're stopping here to let a couple of people off.' I am beside myself with joy. Ya dancer! In free! Kick the can! Ya beauty! The plane landed, after more hand-holding with Duncan. I got my stuff together and started up the aisle, to find *Los Gigantes* blocking it.

'Where are you going, Wee Man?' says one of them. 'You're our mascot. We canna let you leave.'

They kept me on board until they were just about to take the gangway away, ten minutes after the others had left the plane. The stewardesses and the captain thought it was hilarious. They probably put them up to it.

As I trudged eventually up to immigration the officer there said 'Aha, the hitchhiker! Marjory from the SFA is really mad at you for missing your plane.' Ach well, at least I'm back in time to see the wean in the play. When I got home, my wife ushered the kids out of the kichen before turning to me, smiling sweetly and saying with a voice dripping venom. 'Who is this Marjory woman who keeps phoning?'

She still doesn't believe me.

8: Norwegian Woodentops

P.A. Dave is a Plymouth Argyll supporter. He's also as English as snobbery and a vegetarian who loves McDonald's because he thinks their chips are great. He told us that Plymouth Argyll was started by a bunch of Scottish soldiers and that his great-granny had fallen in love with one of them, although she had in fact married a quartermaster from Plymouth.

This is the evidence which he presented to us to support his desire to join the Tartan Army, when he was spotted wearing a tartan tammy with intent in the departure lounge of Glasgow airport. This was in front of an informal tribunal appointed by ourselves to consider his case. It consisted of ourselves and about 50 other people going to faraway places with strange sounding names, some of whom thought we were serious, at least at first. We had an hour or so to kill before the plane left for Oslo so we moved the chairs and tables around to form a military-style court-martial kind of effect. George, Builder John and I were the judges, Anne was the counsel for the defence and Mahoney, who has been in the British Army, and, it didn't surprise any of us to discover, has been on the wrong end of several legal decisions by the military élite, was the prosecution.

His case was succinct. 'He's guilty of being English since before the dawn of time and I ask for a sentence of wire brush and Dettol.' This last, as you probably know, is the reputed army cure for venereal disease, which counts as a self-inflicted wound, apparently, and is an offence against the military rules. Mahoney has had an entire pub full of punters enthralled and aghast with his description of how it had been carried out on him in Malta. 'They pulled the foreskin back. Most people flinch at this, because they pull it back to Cyprus, but not me. I looked the M.O., the manky orifice, in the Japs eye and said "OYAH!!" I didn't flinch, though, but the force of my exclamation did slam several of the people standing in front of me into a wall 50 feet away. No, flinching is for cowards. Shouting "OYAH!!" is the man's way, the soldier's way. I am one of the great "OYAH!!" shouters of all time.'

Each time that Mahoney says 'OYAH!!' during this tale it gets ten decibels louder and it fairly makes him the centre of attention. He went on, 'After they had carried out their self-appointed task, the Medical Officer asked if there was anything that I wanted. "More Dettol," I said unflinchingly, "and you've missed scrubbing one of my testicles. This could be construed as dereliction of duty, sir." As I stood there, holding the tattered shreds of what had been the pride of the whole male side of the Mahoney family, I knew that my irony had struck home, because it was several seconds before they threw me on my back and started again. What annoyed me most was the noise of the power drill with the wire brush attachment, that high pitched, teeth-grinding whine, or maybe that was me.'

He is capable of going on like this more or less forever, depending on the amount of drink taken, and I heard him doing it for a bunch of businessmen and women who had been listening to the trial. One of them patted him on the shoulder and said 'Poor lad'. I'm not sure who was kidding who.

Anne, meanwhile, was defending P.A. vehemently. 'Being English is not a crime,' she stated, holding a finger aloft. 'Yes it is,' said her husband, Builder John, 'objection overruled'. There was muttering from several of the bystanders against this condign condemnation and the ruling was eventually amended to 'Being English is a crime, but only against Scots and anybody else that wants it to be'. One of the English onlookers demurred, saying that it wasn't nearly general enough. George immediately appointed this chap, a well-spoken Englishman in a good suit, *amicus curiae*. 'Scots law or English?' asked the man, who of course turned out to be a lawyer. 'Scots, you Sassenach *scheiss sprecher*,' said George, not knowing what he was talking about. An *amicus curiae*, David told me later (David being the *amicus curiae*) is very different in Scots and English law. In Scots law he is a disinterested observer, not a party to the case. In English law he is counsel acting for a person who is interested in the outcome of a case he is not personally involved in. 'A highly paid Nosey Parker,' said David.

He went immediately into consultation with Anne, who then raised the question of whether you had to be Scottish to be a Scotland supporter. Dave stated loudly that he wanted to be a Scotland supporter but to remain English, especially now that he had met us. This sally was greeted with a few cheers from the audience and Anne pointed out that there were already several precedents. The Darkie asked to be called to give evidence and launched into a convoluted talk of how Princess Anne wants to come to all the Scottish games of football as well as rugby and of how 'they won't let her'. He has advanced this theory several times already in the previous few years and a few times since. He firmly believes it and 'they' have expanded over the years to become a 'concatenation and coalition of Catholics, clowns and catamites', as he has it. Nobody else believes it, but the passionate conviction in his voice swayed the three-man tribunal to grant his wish that the Princess be considered a precedent. Or maybe we just wanted him to shut up.

Then the final statements were made, with Mahoney ending up by asking once again, despite the fact that he thought the defendant should be granted his wish to support Scotland, that the wire brush and Dettol treatment be applied on the grounds that 'a large majority of the people here want to see this happen – especially to an Englishman.' We three then retired from the Bar to the bar, and considered the ramifications of our sentence. We eventually, say 30 seconds later, found the defendant guilty 'of being English and of wearing a tartan tammy without genetic predisposition to do so'. We sentenced him to wire brush and

Dettol 'but only after his death' and to '168 hours of community service, to wit the wearing of said tammy 24 hours a day for one week'. P.A. Dave accepted his sentence with due gravity and carried it out to the letter which meant him wearing it to work in Plymouth for three days. It's not the ideal headgear for the manager of the buying department of Plymouth's biggest store, but he is now called Mad Jock down there, a title of which he is inordinately proud. We offered to call him that too, when he told us, but he declined on the grounds that we were all mad jocks up here, and he wouldn't be unique anymore, so he is stuck with P.A. Dave, or sometimes Pad, as his accent is so thick that it sometimes sounds Irish.

The plane was called and we boarded with our usual roar. I found myself sitting between David the lawyer and John Gregg, as I arrived late for the check-in and got stuck in at the smoking end. After the plane took off, Mahoney, an equally rabid supporter of Celtic and Scotland, came over to talk to big John. Mahoney is an unusual combination for the Tartan Army, as most of the travelling support are not Celtic or Rangers fans, but come from places like Fraserburgh, Ayr, Dumfries and villages and hamlets all over Scotland. Mahoney wanted to tell John about the time the Celtic support cheered him for scoring a goal against them. 'They what?' said John. 'Aye,' said Mahoney, 'I didn't think you'd noticed but it was a big cheer. We were gubbing you three–nil and there were only about five minutes left. You had run your heart out the whole game and wee Bertie Auld was giving you serious verbals, you were not a happy camper. Anyway, you got the ball on the halfway line and everyone in the crowd saw you decide, "Right, I'll show the bastards". You beat three men and crashed it in from about 25 yards. It was a cracker, but the applause was for you, not for the goal. It was just for you, for being you, for never, ever giving up, for playing for the jersey 100 per cent. It was a bit ironic at first but it got louder when we realised we meant it. You were that busy collecting the ball, still trying to rally your team, still thinking you could win, that I didn't think you'd noticed, so I just thought I'd tell you that just for a minute or two we thought you were okay, ya big Proddy bastard.' The Fried Egg looked a bit bemused but said 'Thanks very much', David the lawyer thought that this was great. 'This is what sport is about, the Olympian ideal, play up and play the game,' but big John said 'No it isn't. We still lost, I remember that all right, and I remember scoring the goal, but what I remember most is not winning.'

Two minutes later he was up in the aisle entertaining the company with a tale of when he was playing for Rangers and Scotland, on the top of his game and at the peak of fitness. He got out of the shower at home one day and was posing in front of the mirror, flexing his muscles and glorying in his good health. He padded through to the living room, still naked, and threw a pose in front of his wife. 'Look at that,' he said '200 pounds of male dynamite.' His wife looked pointedly at his wedding tackle and said 'Aye, with a two inch, ten-second fuse'.

The rest of the journey passed in like fashion, with David the lawyer telling us the difference between a road-kill hedgehog and a road-kill lawyer. Apparently there are skid-marks in front of the hedgehog. David left the plane in Copenhagen when we transferred for the plane to Oslo. I never did get his second name, but he told us as he left 'You know, I think I might start supporting Scotland myself'. If you ever read this, David, you'll be welcome, especially in Oslo, where you need to be mega-rich to afford a beer, but more of that later.

When we got to the hotel, the lobby was full of Room Committee guys looking for floor space. George and I were sharing a room but we said we had room for two and a couple of guys who'd come by boat from Edinburgh joined us. They were from Fife and Big Andy was chatting away to them as we got in the lift. No sooner had the door closed when one of them whipped out his John Thomas and started peeing. The guy was mostly drunk but gleeful in that horrible ignorant way, intent on making his mark the only way he knew how. He'd been at it about two seconds, with all of us staring at him appalled, when Andy's hand closed round his throat. 'Stop that, ya low-life,' said Andy 'or I'll rip it off and make you eat it.' The guy actually thought Andy was kidding, so Andy forced his face into the lift carpet and rubbed it in it till it bled, while we held on to his mate. We then took the lift back down and booted them out into the street.

'The thing is,' said Andy, 'they were surprised at us finding it offensive. Did you see that? Fifers, too. Ah well, you and George invited them, so you get to clean the lift.' The receptionist spoke perfect English and George and I explained what had happened, adding that they weren't guests of the hotel and that it was our fault. We offered to wash out the lift but she made that little moue of disgust that women do when they hear of guys peeing anywhere but in a toilet and said that she'd get one of the staff to do it. She did, too, and about 15 minutes later it was all clean and sweet smelling once more. I've never seen either of these two guys again but George and I would like to talk to them, as the hotel charged us 35 quid for cleaning the lift. 'I bet they hope it happens all the time,' said George, as we paid for it.

Then it was the quick shower, into the jerseys and off for a few jars. 'It's six quid a pint,' said Mahoney in greeting us as we went into the lobby. 'Hotels are always dear,' said George, and he was right, as when we got to our designated watering hole we discovered that the lads had negotiated it down to £4.50 by promising not to drink anywhere else. Not that we would have anyway, as the pub was on Karl Johans, the main drag, and it was called The Scotsman. It wasn't changed for our visit, it's always been called that, though there are no Scots working there. The landlord, a healthy looking Nordic chap, must have thought his coupon had come up that week as eventually just about every Scot in Oslo came to the bar. Black Andy was there and for the first time since I've known him, didn't buy a drink for everybody. He's got loads of dough and he's generous with it, but even he balked at laying out a couple of hundred quid for a few beers. Wherever we go he's always got a huge wedge of the local currency, or zobs as we call them. The local currency is always called the zob, for reasons buried in the mists of time, and Andy was decisive 'Too many zobs for me lads. Let's buy our own.' We kittied up and got into finding out what there is to do in Oslo, which is quite a lot if you are into sculpture and the sea, but not very much if you only have four or five grand with you. Oslo's marketing motto is 'You won't believe it', and if they are talking about the prices call me Victor Meldrew. It's a seriously expensive place, which is why we ended up eating at McDonald's, with P.A. Dave as the voice of vegetarianism.

The restaurant manager was a very pleasant no-nonsense lady called Megan from, of all places, Yorkshire. 'Don't go upstairs, lads. There's room in the corner.' There were about eight of us and Dave immediately got the woman's attention. 'Killing animals is wrong,' he said, to an employee of the world's most profitable hamburger chain. 'How do you reconcile that with working here?' The lady was brusque and brisk. 'That's total bollocks, sir,' she said 'I was born, bred and buttered on a farm and I know. Why have you got a Devon accent if you are a Scotland supporter?' As Dave explained we ordered our various Big Macs and stuff and then Megan went away and came back with a vegetarian meal for Dave, with double chips. He hadn't asked for the meal, just the chips, and there wasn't a vegetarian menu, but he tucked in surrounded by slavering carnivores, and seemed to enjoy it. That earned her the title of Vegan Megan and hundreds of customers, once we'd passed the word that she could tell you where everything cheap was in Oslo. She drew up an itinerary for us for the next day and we went back to the hotel for a serious whack at the duty free which most of us had prudently purchased against Nordic strangeness with booze. 'Alcohol will get you through times of no money better than money will get you through times of no alcohol,' said George, downing his third or fourth half-tumblerful of mother's ruin.

Next day we were up relatively bright and very early because we wanted to get at the breakfasts before the other gannets arrived. We had heard tales of meals costing a hundred quid the night before and we wanted to stock up for the day. I noticed a couple of the waitresses staring at us as we attacked the buffet but they were staring even more as we left because we had surreptitiously made up about 50 rolls and sandwiches on sausage and bacon, as well as seriously depleting the butter and jam. Anne was staring at a dinner menu she'd picked up. 'The water is four pounds a bottle. Four pounds for water in a place surrounded by it.' Anne's honesty is legendary but even she filled her tote bag with pieces.

The first stop on Megan's itinerary was a place called Vigeland Sculpture Park which was stuffed full with concrete human figures. There were hundreds of them, old, young, in-between. There were circles of intertwined bodies, clumps, couples, singles and even a huge column about 60 feet high, of naked bodies striving for the top. We are talking serious concrete and sculptural overkill here. Some of them were just ridiculous. There was one of a naked man, balancing on his left leg, engaged in what looks like booting a baby into touch with his right. There were two babies attached to his right forearm with their tiny arms outstretched in Superbabe mode and one falling backwards from a standing position on his left shoulder. The head and arms of the baby attached to the foot are shiny with people rubbing them. Anne read out from a leaflet 'This child is rubbed by Norwegians to prevent premature ejaculation and drowning at sea. It is also believed to be a cure for baldness.' It was a while before we caught on that she was just making it up, as the leaflet was in Norwegian, and Mahoney who has four children of his own, 'or so the wife says', all under seven, looked up at this chap and said with sympathy that sounded real 'I know how you feel, pal'. The sculptor who made them is called Gustav Vigeland and he has created a park of surpassing strangeness. We didn't even go into the museum across the road as it was apparently full of his stuff as well. 'I haven't seen as many stupid statues since I was in George Square,' grumped George, never a man to miss a dig at Glasgow.

Then it was onto the train for a trip to Oslo University, where they have perfected a giant mechanical womb which churns out clones of the perfect 20-year-old Scandinavian woman, or at least that's the way it looks. Anne said the same about the guys. It's a nice relaxing place to wander round in but to George it was a bit like a busman's holiday. 'Students!' he kept saying, 'I came here to get away from students.' Mahoney said, 'And to see Scotland play' and George stared at him for a moment in puzzlement before nodding and agreeing, 'Aye, that too, but it's mostly to get away from students.'

We had broken out the pieces and the nicked orange juices and we were having a picnic on the grass when a wee old man came up to us. 'You Scottish?' he asked, in the accent that breathed over Eden, or at least Priesthill, which was where he was from. As most of us were wearing our jerseys, this didn't take an Einstein to perceive but Archie was well made up. 'Here for the game lads?' he asked rubbing his hands with delight at meeting compatriots.

The Steelman, clad in a complete Scotland strip apart from the boots, explained to Archie that, no, we were actually Norwegian students who'd dressed up and put on Scottish accents for a laugh, almost making Archie and all the rest of us believe it, such is his skill. Then we got to talking. Archie lives all over the place. He's a kind of social worker with the Lapps, who according to him have been royally screwed by generations of Scandinavians. 'They made them into slaves,' he said, with some venom. 'They tried to imprison a free people. They try to keep them from crossing borders which have never existed for the Lapps. The Russians are the worst.' His job is to make sure that nobody, especially the Russians, kills or jails his charges when they merrily herd their reindeer across national frontiers. He's been shot at and threatened dozens of times but he's still at it, a kind of Catcher in the Tundra. He gets them welfare benefits and medical aid and he teaches botany. He was combining some research with a visit to the game and he signed us all into the student bar, where the beer was about half the price it was elsewhere, but you were only allowed to buy two. From the looks he was getting from the students, I suspect that old Archie is a bit of a hero on the side. People kept coming up and shaking his hand. Some of them even asked him to sign their books.

The Steelman noticed this as well and went round the bar collecting donations. 'Lapps, Lapps' he kept saying. He came back just as we were finishing our drinks and dumped around £200 worth of zobs in front of Archie, saying 'Tell them it's from Sanity Clause'. Archie said 'A Sanity Clause is what I'd like to get into the legislation about the Lapps. They get treated a lot worse than the gypsies do at home in Scotland.' This might have something to do with their penchant for smuggling people and stolen furs out of Russia, or with their neat wee trick of circling back on people who annoy or attack them and cutting their throats, but Archie didn't tell us about this until later. George suggested that when Archie phoned his wife to tell her he'd be a bit late that he should say 'I'm just on my last Lapp', and he laughed and agreed. 'I'll just buy the kids some stuff with this,' he said, putting it in his briefcase. He didn't buy toys, though. Anne and John were with him the next day and he bought ribbons, bright thread, beads and hundreds of needles, as well as drawing books and pens.

He asked where we were going next and when we told him that Megan had recommended a couple of museums he went away and came back with some University notepaper on which he wrote something in Norwegian. He said it was an educational discount and it worked. We got 50 per cent off everywhere we went. He also suggested that we visit a couple of his heroes at the Kon-Tiki museum and at one called Polarskifet, so we did. In the Kon-Tiki museum I bought some of the original papyrus reeds from *Ra*, his second boat, the one that Thor Heyerdahl sailed from Morocco to South America just to prove that it could be done, thereby also demonstrating the possibility of Egyptian influence on the Pre-Columbian civilisation of America. It tells me this on the attached card. It is one of my favourite souvenirs and I never look at it without thinking of this Norwegian headbanger tying these reeds together to make a raft you wouldn't sail in the Millport raft race and then launching off into the Atlantic cheerfully confident that he could sail it to where he wanted to. He did too, and because they were replacing the original reeds, I get to relive the journey as often as I want to. It was only two quid and the biggest bargain of the entire trip. Heyerdahl's books about *Kon-Tiki* and *Ra* are superb, genuine real-life adventure for curiosity's sake and a lot of us have read both of them now. Late of an evening, when the talk turns to how we are going to get to South America or wherever for the World Cup after France, we discuss the different properties of the balsa wood logs of *Kon-Tiki* and the reeds of *Ra* with real interest. Oh, to be 20 again. What an adventure that would be.

Near this museum there is another wherein resides *Fram*, a boat about the size of a walnut shell, or at least that's the way it seems. It's about the size of two average living-rooms and it held an entire community of cheerful maniacs, led by the head cheerful maniac, Fridtjof Nansen, who deliberately let the boat be frozen into the Arctic sea to prove a theory about drift and to get him the nearest to the North Pole that anyone had been at that time. This was in the 1890s with no electrics and not much more gadgetry than Columbus had. He succeeded as well. His ship remained uncrushed and he went on to do sterling work for refugees with the League of Nations. He won the Nobel Peace Prize in 1923. They are a curious and very stubborn people, these Norwegians, with a crazy streak a mile across. There's a tape on the *Fram* of what the crushing ice and the groaning timber sound like and it is terrifying, while the boat itself gives you claustrophobia just from looking at it from the outside. The idea of subjecting yourself and your colleagues to this voluntarily is just madness.

As we drifted back onto the boat that had brought us across the bay to the museums, P.A. Dave said that he was hungry and that he was off to McDonald's for some chips. We still had some pieces left and said we'd see him in The Scotsman for a pint. We got there after a pleasant stroll through the older part of the city and were sitting carefully sipping our £4.50 beverages. Counting Jim was saying 'That's ten pence, that's another ten pence,' with every sip, but Andy shut him up. We were talking about our chances in the game next day when P.A. Dave came in, his face a worried mask. He'd been in McDonald's, gone upstairs with his chips and then gone to the toilet, leaving his camera with photos of us that he flatteringly later claimed were priceless, or maybe he meant worthless, and when he came back his camera was gone. He checked with a couple of Scots at the foot of the stairs and no one had gone up or down. This meant that the seven grumpy looking guys in the corner had it. He'd gone over and asked them, but he doesn't speak Norwegian and they pretended not to understand. He'd left the two lads watching the stairs and nicked down to ask our advice, as Megan hadn't been in the restaurant.

Andy, George and I went with him and just as we left the pub we spotted two policepersons, one a young, fresh faced blond chap in his early 20s and the other a woman a couple of years younger who could have been his sister. '*Snakker de Engelsk?*' I asked, showing off one of my half dozen Norwegian phrases. 'Yes, of course we speak English. Can we help you?' answered the young chap. They had the usual continental weaponry – guns, clubs etc. but they seemed very young and innocent to be polis. As we proceeded (in a northerly direction) to the restaurant Dave explained what had happened. They were quiet and courteous, though from a remark one made to the other they obviously thought that he was a bit of an idiot for allowing his camera to be stolen. They had a wee laugh about it but they seemed confident that they could help.

All of that changed when we got to the restaurant. Megan was back, a bit frozen-faced, and she said something to the police that stopped them in their tracks. They both turned frightened eyes to the stairs and when it became obvious that they didn't mean to go up, Andy made a move towards the first flight. The younger cop grasped his arm and said 'No!' sharply. That was the last English we were to hear out of them that night. Andy freed his arm and carried on but George said: 'Hold it, Andy. There's something going on we don't know about.' I'd deduced this as well and turned to ask Megan. As I did so the male cop spoke to her and she went halfway up the stairs and shouted at the guys, who were the only people up there. The police then indicated to us that we should move to the other side of the street from the restaurant door. We did this and the seven scruffiest guys we'd seen in Oslo slouched out. One of them threw something to Dave and both the police jumped back as if they had been burned. It was his film and he turned with it in his outstretched palm to the police in outraged mime. The same guy that had thrown Dave the film shouted something to the police and then turned to wander off with the rest of them. They didn't run and they weren't arrogant or nasty. They just didn't seem to be on the same plane as us. They weren't interested. George moved into professional mode, his voice a middle-class snap, 'Right. They obviously have the camera. Why aren't you arresting them?' but the police were having none of it. The woman was trembling visibly and her mate helped her into their car and got on the radio. I went over to talk to Megan with Dave but she wasn't talking either. She said that we should talk to the police. Andy was outraged, 'Who are these guys, the fucking Untouchables?' he bellowed through the window of the cop car, and he wasn't talking about the police. He got in the back of the car pulling Dave in beside him, but the cops weren't talking.

George and I were exchanging theories. Drugs? Mafia? Undercover cops? None of these guys had ever been a cop. I would have bet money on it. Andy and Dave were by this time singing 'We shall not be moved' and laughing, but the atmosphere in the front of the car was fraught. Suddenly the male cop rounded on Andy and started shouting at him, pointing to his colleague, but it was in Norwegian and we didn't understand. He was still at it when another car, with two older plain clothes officers arrived. They didn't speak English either, they said, which was another lie, as they understood everything we said, and I was beginning to get worried, as was George. They indicated that we should get in the back of their car and we did, a bit reluctantly. After a 20-minute trip we all got out at a huge building that turned out to be police headquarters and after a five minute wait we were asked into the presence of a distinguished man in his late 50s, obviously a very senior cop indeed. He didn't introduce the man behind him but he was obviously a civilian. He didn't speak English either, another lie, and he kept agitatedly interrupting as the cop seated us, asked if we'd like coffee, a cigarette etc. All very urbane and in perfect English. He asked for our names, though he didn't give his, and then said to Dave: 'The camera was of course insured?' Dave shook his head. 'No? That was careless of you. Do you have a receipt for it?' Dave shook his head again. 'Doubly careless. How much was it worth?' Dave said 'Just over £600 plus another £100 for the flash attachment.' The chap said, 'So? Quite expensive' and then he spoke quietly in Norwegian to the guy with him. Then, after the guy had replied in the affirmative, he turned to Dave and said 'To business then. You have not yet made an official complaint and we have received no report. Do you wish to do this? Wait before you answer. The gentleman with me is from the city government and he wishes to pay you compensation for your camera of the amount you suggested. Seven hundred and fifty of your pounds in kroner. Well?' Just as Dave said, 'I'll take it,' George said 'What exactly is going on?' and the urbane gent said 'We would ask you not to speak of this while you are here. Not to your friends or to anyone else. We do not wish to discuss it further and the offer depends on you keeping your mouths closed.' Dave said again, 'I'll take it,' and made a key-turning gesture on his lips. Then he turned and presented the other guy with the imaginary key.

The besuited city official gestured to Dave to come with him and Andy went too. The policeman rose from his desk and signed that George and I should follow him, but we stayed in our seats and George asked yet again, 'What exactly is going on?' The guy hummed and hawed but eventually he realised that we weren't leaving without an explanation. He finally said: 'These men are junkies, drug addicts.' George said 'So, Edinburgh's full of them and we don't piss our pants when we see them. What's the problem?' I said 'Glasgow too,' before I'd thought about it. This Glasgow–Edinburgh thing between George and me is getting out of hand. The cop went on 'They are needle users and they have the Plague.' He said it as though The Plague had huge capital letters. 'Don't be stupid,' said George, 'No one has bubonic plague anymore. What are you talking about?' 'No,' said the cop quietly. 'They have' and he paused dramatically 'AIDS!' George and I laughed out loud. 'You would not be laughing if you were that young policewoman. She is several months pregnant and she is afraid. These men have threatened many of my officers with needles.' This of course was some years back and Aids information was not as widespread as it is now. These junkies were using the only weapon at their disposal to hold the city to ransom. In their ignorance of the odds against getting Aids, the cops were paralysed. George asked, 'Are they homosexual?' and the cop sat down opposite us again. 'We think that two of them are and that they infected the others. The others know this it seems, but it does not appear to matter to them.' George asked 'Why don't you arrest them?' and the cop shrugged and said 'They don't commit violent crimes and they are always together. They do not steal much as they have state support. Our state benefits here are quite large and they have also a house that one of them owns. If we try to arrest them all at once one of my men might be infected and that would be impossible. I could not ask them to do that and besides their union would not allow it. Worst of all if I did order them to arrest these men many would refuse and that also would be impossible.'

George and I made several suggestions, including gassing their house. George suggested snipers. When he caught me looking at him a bit askance he said: 'With anaesthetic darts, of course.' The cop, who by this time had refused point blank to tell us his name or his rank, said 'But they have not really committed any crimes, at least nothing much. They are ill. It is not right that they should not be punished but they have The Plague. We are waiting for legislation to arrive. In the meantime we do not want anyone to know that in Oslo we cannot deal with this. We do not want every junkie and Aids person to come here.'

'Aha!' thought George and I looking at each other as the penny dropped. 'You don't need to worry about Oslo becoming the Aids capital of Europe,' I said, 'Edinburgh already has that title.'

'We know,' said the high heid polis 'and we have talked long about this. You are from Edinburgh?' This was to me and I said 'I would rather stick, if you'll excuse the expression, dirty needles in my eyes.'

George was consoling. 'It's not really a problem for us and the police in Edinburgh. Surely you have spoken to them?'

'We have,' said the cop, 'but the people in Edinburgh do not seem to be afraid in the way people in Oslo are. It is a big problem. People are afraid. Here and in America also. The people do dreadful things. It is a very, very worrying thing.' He was telling us, in all seriousness, I think, of a plan which had been put forward by a Norwegian MP to isolate all Aids cases on an island, when Dave and Andy returned, both grinning widely. Dave patted his pocket and stuck up his thumbs. 'Let's go for a beer.' The policeman shook hands all round, a bit reluctantly with George, I thought, and got a driver to take us back to The Scotsman in a van. 'Please tell no one,' he said, and Dave did his mouth-key thing again. As we got out of the van Dave gave George and I 50 quid each in zobs. Andy already had his. 'You'll need it for another camera,' said George and Plymouth Argyll Dave said in an accent as thick as clotted cream, 'I've got me priceless pictures of you lot and these Norwegian woodentops have just given me £600 more than I paid for the camera. I hope to Christ they don't find it before we leave. The first round is on me.' And we gubbed their team next night as well.

9: Slavonski Brod and the
Magic Eye

I would rather be a Croat than a Serb
I would rather be a Croat than a Serb
I'd rather be a Croat, rather be a Croat
Rather be a Croat than a Serb.

We'd tried it the other way round in the hotel bar in Zagreb the
night before, as in 'I'd rather be a Serbo than a Croat,' but the
hotel manager, the only man we'd met in Zagreb who spoke one
word of English had very kindly suggested that we did not sing it
in his hotel. 'Or what?' said Cross Kris. 'Or my brother-in-law will
shoot you,' said the nice man, smiling broadly. He suggested that
if we did sing it, it would sound better the other way round and
went away, smiling quietly to himself.

This was in 1989, when Yugoslavia was Yugoslavia and Croatia,
Serbia, Bosnia and the others had not been heard of in Scotland.
We were not unaware that something unpleasant was going on, as
several of us had felt bad vibes and we'd seen several fist fights, but
we had no inkling of the catastrophe that was about to engulf the
area a few months hence. We were on a train from Zagreb, in the

heart of Croatia, heading for Slavonski Brod to support the Under-21 team evermore.

There were about 40 of us, the usual suspects, and the hotel manager had organised a carry-out and a picnic for us, all neatly labelled with the ingredients of the sandwiches. 'What's in this?' asked George as he took a huge bite out of one. I'm the translator again and I got out my *Serbo Croat for Travellers*. Mahoney grabbed it and turned to the food section. 'What's it say?' he asked. George said something like 'lossos'. 'Right,' said Mahoney, 'that's thinly sliced and pickled snake's testicles.' George took another big bite. 'Is that what it is? It tastes a bit like fish.' Mahoney was equally inventive with the other sandwiches. Mine, which I'm sure was roast beef with some kind of vinegary mustard, he described as 'goat arse with sea cucumber vomit'.

The train took hours and we whiled away the time by making up songs, telling stories, commenting on the flat-to-the-horizon countryside and drinking the excellent Zagreb beer we'd been provided with. We'd expected it to last the journey, but then we'd expected to get seats on the train, having paid for them, but it was full to bursting with soldiers in various kinds and colours of uniforms, all armed to the teeth. Some of them had three or four handguns strapped to themselves and a lot of them had machine guns, so we weren't feeling much like demanding our rights.

Cross Kris and Bodyswerve returned from an expedition up the train to announce that there was a bar and we set off, struggling through the crush of men and sharp metal. When we got to the bar it was more packed than the rest of the train but about ten minutes after we got there the train stopped and all the guys in the brown uniforms got off, leaving us plenty of room. We delivered ourselves of yet another chorus of 'I'd rather be Croat' to announce our presence and the barman said: 'That is a good song to sing on this train. Do not sing it anywhere else.' We still didn't understand and we sang it with great success all over the place in Slavonski Brod later on, but I'm getting ahead of myself.

Cross Kris, who is actually Swiss, despite being a rabid Hibee and having an Edinburgh accent that you could sharpen steel on, is demanding my translation services. He is called Cross Kris because, as well as being a cross-dresser, that is, he always wears his

Hibs shirt under his Scotland top, he is also a specialist in winding up the opposition. He's as pleasant and gentle a man as you'll meet, but at the games he turns into a raging maniac, screaming vituperation at both sides. He wants to know the Serbo-Croat word for 'foul' and phrases like 'headbanging eejit' and 'dirty bastard'. None of them were in my book so I turned to the barman for help. His English was okay, if a bit limited, so I introduced Kris to him and sat and listened. The barman was called something like Mirk and as I flicked through the pages of my phrase book I became aware that Kris wasn't the only one at the wind-up. I'd learned quite a few words over the last few days and Mirk was explaining to Kris that *'krompir a cevapicici'* meant 'kill the bastard'. Kris was writing it down phonetically and also learned to shout *'Merkvah'* for 'foul' and *'kakavaly'* for 'referee'. He spent the rest of the train journey learning them and a few others and during the game he went mad with them. I had a word or two myself with Mirk after consulting my book and discovered that when Kris thought he was shouting 'Kill the bastard,' he was actually bawling 'potatoes and mince balls'. Every foul was 'carrot' and the referee was a particularly nice cheese. He also shouted 'I'm a homosexual' at every corner for the Scots. I didn't tell Kris this but I did pass it on to a selected few friends (i.e. everybody else), and it fair brightened up the game for us. Kris found out months later and dropped me a wee postcard from Switzerland suggesting that I come and visit him but that before doing so I should learn phrases in Swiss like 'Where is the hospital' and 'Can you remove this rifle from my rectum'. His plans for Mirk sound really painful. The Swiss government gave Kris his rifle and insists that he keep it at home. Every male Swiss has one and Kris says that it is a very polite country.

As the train drew into Slavonski Brod and its ten yards of platform, we found ourselves miles away from it and had to jump the three or four feet down onto weeds and jaggy rocks. You couldn't see the jaggy rocks for the weeds but gravity helped us find them. We assembled the squad and went looking for Yugoslavia's most important product. Wherever we go in the world it is the first and often only word everybody learns. In Yugoslavia it is *'pivo'*. I gathered my few scraps of Serbo Croat and approached a middle-aged man who had also got off the train, but at the platform, sure proof that he was local. As I opened my mouth everybody behind me starting shouting '*pivo!*' and pointing to their gaping mouths like a bunch of starving chicks in a nest. 'Da, da,' he said and led us to a bar and restaurant about 200 yards up a steep hill and a particularly unappetising street, all concrete blocks of flats and a distinct lack of street furniture, like lights or pavements. 'It looks a bit like Bellshill,' said somebody. 'But without the international ambience,' said somebody else.

In the bar we bought our new friend a *pivo* and I asked him if he could show us a place to eat later. He suggested that right here was as good as any place and introduced us to the owner, a laughing man who was uncrating a small Japanese TV. Bodyswerve took over the installation, as it's one of the things that he does for a living. They were chatting away to each other, understanding not a word between them and once Bodyswerve had it tuned in and Bro the owner was pushing buttons on it, he came over and said quietly to the Steelman and me: 'He doesn't know that it's a remote control.' He passed the little black box to the Steelman and he took off quietly round the guys looking for batteries. He came back and we tried it out quickly when no one was looking. It worked.

I was then faced with one of my most difficult translation feats ever. I shouted Bro over and explained with much pointing out of words in the book that the Steelman had a magic eye that could switch the TV on and off. The Steelman pointed to his right eye, which is a guileless pale blue, just like his other one. Both are totally misleading. He winked slowly and the TV went off. Bro jumped up and shouted something as the Steelman winked again and it went on. I then explained that he could also do channels and everybody in the bar learned the Serbo Croat for the numbers one to ten as the Steelman blinked away like a semaphore sending an urgent message. It had become clear that Bro did not know even the concept of remote control and when he shouted something else his wife came through from the back, listened to his excited explanation, had her very own demonstration then made an odd kind of fork thing with her fingers at the Steelman and fled through to the kitchen. Bro was out at the door, shouting to a couple of passers-by. They came in and got their own free show. After about ten minutes we had every granny and grandpa from the area in the bar, crossing themselves and staring at the Steelman. People even turned away when he looked at them.

A wee boy of about nine or ten came in with his schoolbag and went through to the kitchen, only to reappear in about a minute with his mum. He was angry because we had frightened her and he walked up to the Steelman and mimed pressing a remote control while yelling at him as his mum and dad tried to shush him. Big Andy gave the boy the device and as he demonstrated it to his parents there were gasps and relieved smiles.

Andy and I mimed drinks for everybody and the Steelman gave the boy the equivalent of about a pound. The wee guy was delighted and was now totally in charge of the remote control. Bodyswerve showed him how the batteries went in and how to tune the telly to different channels. We made it clear that none of the old people were allowed to put their hands in their pockets and that we'd buy them as much to eat and drink as they wanted. That started the party. It was still only about four o'clock and hours till the game started. The local people kept slipping out and coming back with their traditional dresses and jackets on. Then they started showing us their dancing. They had accordions, small things, and we showed them the Highland Fling (Lowland version, involving much shouting of '*Teeyeuch*!' and not a lot of grace or style, but bags of enthusiasm).

Builder John, Anne and a couple of the others know steps to lots of Scottish country dances and before you could say 'Jesus, I'm fleeing and my feet are boufing,' everybody was at it. If you weren't dancing you were shouting and singing nonsense words. The Monster from Maryburgh didn't have his own box with him, but he picked up playing their wee accordion quickly and their musicians picked up our tunes.

Bro produced a guitar and spoke to all the local people seriously. They all stood up and took their hats off and so did we. Everybody was staring solemnly into space as Bro sang a song that must have lasted seven or eight minutes, with much gesturing and wiping of pretend tears. I noticed that a few of the younger guys and girls in their lot were looking a bit rigid and there seemed to be rather a lot of wee grins being exchanged but it wasn't till he went to sing it again that everybody burst out laughing. We'd all been standing at attention, trying to look interested, while he sang the Serbo Croat equivalent of 'Baa Baa Black Sheep'. We had happened across a kindred spirit, a man for whom the wind-up was a way of life.

Bro's wife was by this time cooking up a storm and huge bowls of delicious food kept arriving. The Yugoslavs kept nipping out and coming back with jars of pickled walnuts and gherkins and all sorts of other things. While we ate, they sang, and we passed around bottles of wine, beer and something that turned out to be apricot brandy. By the time kick-off time was approaching I was full to bursting.

George was busy trying to pay the bill, which Bro's wife and son had been keeping a less than assiduous eye on. They wrote it on a huge sheet of paper on one of the tables and a few of the guys felt that they were forgetting to add items. 'They're cheating themselves,' said Peter, who is called Storchy, or the Battery Boy for reasons he does not wish to discuss but which we do, often, much to his embarrassment, in female company. Peter's distinguishing ploy as a Motherwell supporter was to take an inflatable Pope, for which he had bought a seat, to Ibrox, and on being challenged by a steward, to loudly defend his right to do so. It took four of them, in ascending order of seniority, to convince him that this was not Plan A, survival-wise. He deflated it for the game but blew it up again afterwards and is fondly remembered for bursting into the Railway Bar in Motherwell shouting 'The Huns have kidnapped the Pope!'

George came over from this discussion saying: 'It only seems to come to about 70 quid for all of us. They are definitely doing themselves and Bro won't take any money just now, anyway. A lot of them are coming to the game with us and we're to pay after the game.'

Off we went, accompanied by most of the people in the bar. The stadium was a major surprise, as it was as bad as the worst of Scotland's junior parks, with a stand that held about 100, a few desultory sleepers for terracing across from the stand and just grassy banks at either end.

As history sadly records, we got gubbed 4–1 though it wasn't a bad game. During it, while Cross Kris was doing his Viking berserker shouting things, the Yugoslavs found out that one of them, aided by me, had set him up for it and at each cry of 'carrot' or 'I'm a poof', they fell about. Kris didn't notice, nor did he notice the two very drunk, blue-clad headbangers who were going to attack him. Bro and Andy and not a few of the others grabbed them and starfished them, two to a limb. If you thought my description of the soldiers sounded worrisome, you should have seen the police. These guys clanked when they walked and they were built like tanks. When the heavies arrived Bro and the others explained what had happened and without further ado the cops got laid into the two guys with batons and feet. Then they frog-marched them away, still whanging them with their huge batons, to their van. 'Bad Blue Boys,' said one of the Yugoslavs in English. He didn't speak any other English but I found out the next day that Dinamo Zagreb's casuals are called Dinamo Bad Blue Boys – in English. It is written on walls all over town. Storchy was with me when I discovered one and he said 'Fuck me, even the Yugoslavs have got Huns.'

After the game we went back to Bro's place, to be met by everyone we'd already met before, plus about another 50 very old people. I asked if they had gone to an old people's home and invited them and was understood, because by this time we'd met a guy whom everybody called Dobar Dan. It means 'hello' in Serbo Croat but he didn't seem to mind us calling him that and he spoke a bit of English and fluent French. When I asked this Mrs Bro stared at me oddly and Dobar Dan did the same. He then explained that the concept of an old people's home didn't sit well with the people of Yugoslavia, that there wasn't one in Slavonski Brod and that Mrs Bro had just said there never would be. These were just people from round about, here with their children and grandchildren. Anne said, 'And we call ourselves civilised!'

On the way to the game we had captured an Englishman, Man U Mike, now a regular attender with us. He was standing on his own in the main street wearing a Scotland top and looking a bit apprehensive. His accent is pure Manchester and there is nothing remotely Scottish about him. Yea, nothing unto the umpteenth generation. He'd just decided that he'd had enough of supporting England. He'd had it with the yobbery and the tabloid press attitude to the fans in England. A couple of the lads had interrogated him in friendly fashion as we walked back from the game, where he had been mega-impressed with the way the Bad Blue Boys had been dealt with, and they reported that he was solid.

He was looking even more worried now because the Steelman had been filling his head with stories of our elaborate initiation rites and telling him that joining the Masons or the US Marines was a doddle compared to signing up with the Tartan Army. The Steelman explained that it works as follows. What you do is invent your own initiation rite or torture. If we don't think it is nasty or humiliating enough, then we do our own. You have to write down the suggestions and we pass them round. If we accept yours the last person to read it hands it back to you and it is carried out. If we don't the last person tears up your note and then our torment is visited on you sometime in the next 24 hours. Some of them have been pretty horrible and Mike's was a cracker, but we passed it round and George, with Mike looking on, collected all our negative headshakes and ceremoniously tore up Mike's paper.

You could see him brace himself, but the joke is that the next 24 hours is actually the initiation ceremony. We never do anything. We just let them sweat about what could be worse than what they had already suggested. One guy in Mexico suggested something quite easy, ten push-ups or something like that, and ran for it when we tore up his paper. We haven't seen him since. Mike was game, but Mahoney and Sweeney, the Tim Twins, fairly got him going. Mahoney said meaningfully 'English, eh?' and wandered back to the bar, while Todd had a group together muttering and glancing over darkly at Mike.

While this was going on, the grandmother of all hooleys was gaining momentum. The fun was getting loud and the liquor was flowing. Two polis turned up at the door with a message from the polis at the game thanking us for our help. They said that the Bad Blue Boys would be sent away to some kind of court or encouraged to join the army. I think that this policy probably had something to do with the horrors that have afflicted Yugoslavia since. At the big game in Zagreb the police guarded *us* against *them*, and there weren't any real problems, but these guys were headbangers squared and cubed and as mindless as any fascist stormtrooper.

George had finally got the bill for the evening organised and it only came to about five or six pounds a head, so George suggested a tenner and everybody chipped in. We told Dobar Dan to tell Bro to buy stuff for the old people with the excess. They rejected this suggestion and Anne said we should put it towards the wee boy's education. This met with general approval, particularly from Mr and Mrs Bro and suddenly everybody was kissing everybody else. We got them all in a circle and sang 'Auld Lang Syne'. The accordionist knew the tune, a tribute to the ubiquity of Burns. As we started on it, by popular demand, for about the third time, Bro suddenly shouted '*Vlak, Vlak,*' their word for train. George usually has us well organised but he and an old granny lady had been hammering the gin and he was a bit wandered. We all pelted down the unlit street with the cops leading the way in their car and we got to the station just as the train arrived. We all clambered on, trying to persuade a few of them to come with us, but they declined, smiling.

As the train pulled out we discovered why they were smiling, because they all started pointing the other way. They had put us on a train heading away from Zagreb toward some unknown hinterland. Instant panic, because the game was the next day. Some of the group were for jumping off because it wasn't going very fast but it was pitch black and you couldn't see what you were jumping onto. As the hysteria mounted, the train stopped and backed up to the station again, where what looked like the entire town were falling about pissing themselves laughing. Bro and his wee boy were leaning on each other, exhausted with mirth, taking turns to point the telly remote control at us.

Our proper train wasn't for another 40 minutes and the crowd had brought us some crates of the local beer, so we lit a big fire by the railroad track and danced 'Auld Lang Syne' around it. I've never heard it sung with more fervour and it was a magic end to a very special day with some special people.

Slavonski Brod was damaged very badly during the various battles and a lot of people were killed. There is an orphanage there now which has been helped by a charity called aftaCARE. One of the other things that it does is to bring a coachload of children from the region to Britain for a holiday twice a year, in late July for three weeks, and at Christmas. They could use money and they are also actively looking for host families all over Britain.

The address for donations is aftaCARE, 28 The Green, Brill, Buckinghamshire HP18 9RU and its secretary, Margaret Behan, will answer queries during office hours on 01865 794714.

10: La Bateria

Builder John was recounting for the first time what is now one of his favourite tales. 'It was in Acapulco, and we were sharing the hotel with the English mob. We were having a great time but they just didn't seem all that friendly, you know. They're a bit like the Germans, always got to be first and best. Think they're God's gift.' We were in the bar in Nezahualcoyotl which is imaginatively named La Cantina and heads were nodding at this assessment. We do try not to be anti-English but with some of them it really is difficult.

Big Andy gave up going to Wembley, like most of us, because it is amateur talent night for the anti-English brigade who come out of the woodwork with their stupid and racist taunts, but even he used to have a big badge that said 'I hit people who call me Jock'. He's saying, 'Yeah, remember that time going to Wembley? Those two wifies were scared to death of us and we were just trying to be nice. I'm not travelling 600 miles to be treated like a beast.' One of Andy's claims to fame is that he was 'first man on the crossbar, that was me', after the '77 Wembley game when we laughingly went over the walls, dug up pieces of turf and took the goalposts apart. I've met at least 20 people who have corner flags from the game and half a dozen who claim to have snaffled the hare that the greyhounds chased. Everybody has their own tale of that game. It was vandalism without doubt, but there was no mindless malice involved. It was simply souvenir-hunting taken a bit beyond normal bounds by excitement and triumph and the reaction of the English press is still deeply resented by the Tartan Army.

'It's true enough,' said John, 'their papers tend to make us sound like we're savages. But then they do that with their own supporters.'

'Aye, but some of their supporters are monsters right enough,' said Mahoney, who had met a few whom he had not liked at all during the last campaign. We all have our own share of guilty past in our older and not all that wiser days and we have known Scottish monsters too, but we like being thought of as 'the best behaved supporters in the land' and we take care to try to uphold our reputation. 'Anyway,' continued John, 'there wasn't any aggro, no violence, just the odd wee niggle. They were awfy territorial about one particular pub in Acapulco and this wee old guy from Glasgow didn't know this and he sat down there for a beer and a rest. They called him Jock and made sure that he felt unwelcome so after about ten minutes he just up and left. But he was not a happy camper.' Anne took up the tale. 'His name was Jimmy and he was one of these guys who doesn't say much – in fact you'd think words were a fiver each the way he spoke, but he came into his own with the buses.'

The buses were a bit of a cause for upset in Acapulco. Scotball, the SFA travel organisation, had them laid on for travellers with them but there were more than a few who hadn't booked with them and Scotball were digging in their heels a bit over taking them to the games, so the group went and tried to book their own bus, only to discover that the English supporters had commandeered every bus within a 50 mile radius. Some of the guys approached them for a lift to somewhere where they could get a bus or train to Mexico City but it was no go. 'We'd have given them a lift – in fact we did give an older English couple a hudgie – but they just said no,' said John, 'and then they started taunting the group that had asked them. "Walking it, are you Jock?" and "No room for Jocks on our bus" were some of the things they were shouting,' said John.

Anne went on. 'Some of the boys were sitting around talking aggro but Jimmy came over and said "Ignore them," and walked away. He had been beavering away behind the scenes and eventually Scotball took everybody who wanted to go. But Jimmy wasn't finished. "Will we be going in a convoy with the English?" he was asked. "No" he replied, "I think you'll find that that won't be the case".' Anne was laughing at the memory as John took up the story. 'Getting information out of him was like pulling teeth, but when the time to leave came in the morning and we were on our buses we could all see the English milling about waiting for theirs.'

'And they waited a long time,' laughed Anne, 'Jimmy phoned from the hotel the night before with a Mexican guy he had met who didn't like the English either and cancelled all of their buses. It cost some of them megabucks in taxis to get to their game.' John was laughing and asked Anne: 'Do you remember what he said when he got on the bus?' 'Aye,' she said, 'he tapped his nose and said, "Revenge is a dish best eaten cold". Then he said, "Yum Yum", and rubbed his stomach and everybody started laughing.'

Everybody in La Cantina, which means 'The Pub', was laughing by this time, including the very few people from Neza who looked as if they could afford a drink. We'd set up a tab, but the prices were ridiculously low. I'd been first in and gone up to the bar and demanded the cheapest drink in the place in a loud voice. Mahoney and The Darkie were with me and we all got a half-tumbler full of stuff called *pulche*, pronounced 'poolkay'. I tell you the pronunciation so that you will never risk drinking it. It is made from the fermented juice of a plant called *maguey*, which is I think a kind of cactus and tastes like the stuff that you paint on your nails to stop you biting them. It cost about six pence for the three of us and we were robbed. It gave the Mexicans a laugh, though, as it claps your jaws in and you behave like the young tenderfoot on every Western movie who has just been given his first shot of rotgut whisky.

I'd been practising my Spanish on the bartender and I'd asked him what people in Mexico drink. 'If you are poor, *pulche*, Señor Escothes. If you are *un richacho* [a dirty capitalist] then you drink champagne from the slippers of whores.' This Señor Escothes was a funny thing. It means Mr Scottish and they called all of us that. The Danes, who we were playing that day, were called Señor Danés. They treated us like minor princes and they were just about the nicest people in Mexico, despite living in a howling wilderness of a slum.

Enrique the barman was a fount of knowledge about Mexican drink and social customs. He thought that the entire government from the post office clerks on up should be taken out and shot. There had been some kind of student unrest the night before in Mexico City centre and he was angry about it. He also taught all of us to make a clip-clopping noise with our tongues if we wanted a *dos equis*, a fairly expensive (for Mexico) but truly excellent beer. It means 'two horses' he told us, but I've since discovered that it means 'two Xs', so maybe he was sending us up. No one else in Mexico seems to know that this clucking noise means beer.

A whole bunch of Danes had come in to La Cantina about an hour earlier and while they didn't have the tartan to fall back on, they nevertheless were a pretty colourful and cheery bunch. They had come in singing, 'We are red. We are white. We are Danish dynamite' to the tune of 'The Caissons Go Rolling Along' and we had replied with our traditional and deeply poetic 'You can stick your fucking bacon up your arse', to the tune of 'She'll Be Coming Round The Mountain', at which they had laughed a lot.

I asked one of them why they sang in English and he said 'If we sang it in Danish, only we would understand it'. We got them to do it and they were right. They then asked for a song in Scottish and The Steelman obliged with that one about the wee boy, his farra, a barra, an arra and a sparra. The Dane I was talking to said, 'Scottish language is very different from English'. Their equivalent of the English are the Swedes and it would be a brave man who called a Dane a Swede. One of them told us a long story about a Dane who was mistaken for a Swede. It ends up 'but I'm not a Swede. I've been very ill, you blind bastard.' The Danes thought it was hilarious but it may have lost something in the translation.

It was now getting near game time and the adrenalin was beginning to flow. Our battle chant for that campaign was 'Everywhere We Go', which you could hear all over Mexico City the night before and it was filling the air of Neza.

Everywhere we go-o!
People want to know-ow
Who the hell we a-are
And where do we come from
Pause, then (*molto fortissimo*)
We're the Tartan Army
We're mental and we're barmy
Oh oh oh oh
Oh oh oh Scotland! Da da ra ra, Scotland!
We'd walk a million miles for one of your goals
Oh, Sco-o-otland!

This is an audience response chant. You sing the first line and the audience repeats it. It's a brilliant device for getting foreigners to join in the singing and the Danes were soon 'Oh, oh, ohing' along, except that of course they were substituting Denmark for Scotland. George made up a song with several verses that went to their tune. One of them was 'We wear tartan. We're not spartan. And I'm Dolly fucking Parton. Na Na Na Na, Na Na Na, Na Na.' As we were all laughing along together a couple of young Neza boys had come up to me. We were preparing to leave and I wasn't really listening closely. Enrique was frowning at them and waving them away with his fingertips, shooing them off, but one of them said 'We'll see you here after the game,' and I, proud of having understood, said we would.

On the way down to the game we, like the Danes, were appalled at the conditions these people lived under. Enrique's bitterness at the government was easy to understand, as this place is the pits. I've been told that there are much worse places but I hope I never see them. Then we got to the stadium, which is lush and green and obviously costs a fortune to maintain. I don't know if a Mexican team plays there but if one does I hope that it's a good one, as the people of Nezahualcoyotl deserve better than the economic catastrophe around them.

Before the game there were all sorts of pageants and a re-enactment of some Aztec legends involving young boys and girls in swimsuits and full body gold paint. They were put on by local people and they were rigidly determined to get every word and gesture over clearly. They'd obviously been practising for months and it was very moving watching their dedication to explain the history of their people to a bunch of beer-sodden eejits from two countries they'd never ever get the chance to visit.

There were official parades of neatly dressed young people and groups of wee boys in what were obviously supposed to be the various national strips. All of Grupo E, *El Grupo de Muerte* (the Group of Death), were represented and the wee girl at the head of our representatives was carrying a Saltire in a rather electric shade of blue and wearing a MacGregor tartan shirt that looked like it had been made from a tablecloth. They did their best by us and they did us proud. Our lot all stood to attention and saluted as they went past and so did the Danes, so we did it for their flag as well. The Mexicans just loved it and they cheered and clapped and passed sweeties around. It's a charming custom, this thing with the sweeties. All the kids do it and so do a lot of adults. When they meet each other in the street they shake hands and then unwrap a caramel and pop it into the pal's gob. The dentists in Mexico probably make a fortune, except that none of these people looked as if they ever owned a *peso*, never mind enough money to go to the dentist.

As we went into the ground the few smiling cops didn't seem to be bothering with all this segregation nonsense so the Danes we'd been with and another dozen or so of their compatriots came in with us. I reckon that there were maybe 3,000 Scots in the ground and about 1,000 Danes, with possibly 2,000 or 3,000 locals, including the Mexican boys in their Scottish and Danish kit. They cheered for the side whose top they had on and the rest of the local folk took sides with whoever they were standing next to.

I plumped myself down on the stone seats, just drying out from the mini shower that seems to happen at 3 p.m. in Mexico City every afternoon, and found myself sitting next to a pleasant and chatty English woman. I asked her what she was doing there and she said 'I'm with him,' pointing to a tall, balding sunburnt guy. It was Jack Charlton, over checking out Scotland, who were part of Ireland's opposition for the next European championships. He hadn't officially started with Ireland yet and Mrs Charlton told me that he had paid for the trip out of his own pocket. No wonder he's such a good manager. Ireland gubbed us at Hampden and held us to a draw in Dublin in the qualifiers so for him it was money well spent. He also provided free advice to the Scottish team. Loudly. All through the game. Non-stop. His wife smiled fondly at him as he dispensed commands like. 'In hard! Get him!' and criticisms like 'Ballwatching'. We had a chat about tactics with him at half-time and he just thinks in terms of defence, really. 'Everything starts from the back,' he said, as a former England centre-half and World Cup winner would, I suppose. I happen to disagree with him totally as I would rather watch 11 goal scorers than 11 stoppers and I said as much. 'Your team doesn't seem to agree,' he said, beetling his brows at me fiercely. He's a passionate man, Jack Charlton, and difficult to disagree with; but most of the football his team play is stultifyingly boring and not my idea of what I want to watch. I'd rather see us lose with style than win by hacking people to the ground, and most of us think the same. He thinks exactly the opposite and he turned the footballing destiny of an entire nation around and brought joy and excitement to millions of people, but he hadn't done that yet at this point so we all argued away, more or less amicably, until the second half started.

We won the first half, no doubt about it, and the football both sides was playing was a joy to watch, with Charlie Nicholas swivelling and feinting like the world class player he almost became before Arsenal and London combined to take the edge off him. He nearly scored a couple of times, once from a Gough header and once from a Strachan cross. Gough himself nearly scored with a header and then blew the best chance of the game by beasting the ball over the bar from a Strachan pass. There was also a fair bit of stick being handed out, mainly by the Danes, and Aitken and Strachan got clattered both over and off the ball.

It was 0–0 at half time and the Danes changed tactics on the restart with Laudrup lying deeper and prompting breaks. Willie Miller was playing like a champion but after his fifth or sixth game-saving tackle the ball broke off him and their striker whacked it in off the post. Scotland seemed to tire more quickly as the game went on and the Danes contained us well despite Big Jack's urgent and very loud advice: 'Drop it in the corners! Make them run!'

With about ten minutes to go Charlie Nicholas was brutally ambushed from behind by a challenge that wouldn't have looked out of place in a needle Junior derby match in Ayrshire. It was not so much a tackle as an assault with a deadly weapon, to wit Klaus Bergreen's right boot, and he should have been off the field and banned for the rest of the tournament. He only got booked, though, and Jack said, 'His man might have scored' but he did have the grace to look a bit shamefaced and he agreed that he should have been sent off. Nicholas was off, ankle ligaments totally *kaput*, and he missed the rest of the tournament.

When the whistle finally went the Danes were yumping with yoy, as my wee flaxen-headed pal Jesper pronounced Yesper, might have said, but they had taken the no-doubt-they-thought prudent precaution of nipping forwards ten or 15 yards and our black looks bounced off ecstatic, bounding, red-clad backs. Jesper and three or four of the others approached us to shake hands and as he came up to Andy he popped a sweetie into Andy's mouth. Andy had been doing a creditable impression of not so much a storm cloud as a major hurricane but when Jesper did this he smiled and held out his hand. 'Sorry you lost,' said Jesper, a nice thing to say and one we probably wouldn't have thought of if the score had been the other way round, which it could have been if it wasn't for the fact that by historic footballing evidence, God is an Englishman (or woman: *pace* my feminist friends).

They had won their first-ever game in their first ever World Cup Finals and they deserved their moment, so we gave them a clap and we all marched back to La Cantina singing, via yet another pageant from the local people. These Danes were anything but gloomy and they soon joshed us out of our own depression. They even came up with a chant to encourage us in Queretaro. 'If you hate the fucking Germans clap your hands,' so we were all agreed about something.

Jan and Jesper, or Yan and Ying, as George called them, as Jan is about 6ft 3in and dark and Jesper is blond and 5ft 6in, had come up with this plan to give money to the people in Neza. They wanted to start a school. This seemed like a good idea and our money was burning guilty holes in our first-world pockets as we looked around us. When we got to the bar we put this to Enrique but he said 'No. A school is wherever you want it to be. We need money to pay the teacher's wages and we have none, so we teach ourselves. If you want to give your money away, give it to anybody you see. Everyone will take pleasure in it and some will truly need it.'

We decided that we would start redistributing our wealth by giving some to Enrique in exchange for *dos equis* and we were all clucking away like demented chickens, when one of the young guys who had been trying to attract my attention before the game finally succeeded in escaping Enrique's eagle and paternalistic eye. He had heard me asking for the cheapest thing they had and he heard me asking for it in Spanish. We always ask for the cheapest thing wherever we go, in the local language if we can, because sometimes it tastes great and it's always good to let people know that you are not made of money. Young Juanito was rabbiting away but I was only understanding about one word in three. I slowed him down eventually and we bought him a *dos equis*, his first I suspect, while we worked out what he wanted.

What he wanted was to help us. He knew of something cheaper than *pulque*. Given that enough *pulque* to split your skull and stick your tongue to your upper palate forever could be bought for around ten pence, this sounded like an opportunity. 'Less dear?' I asked. 'Si, si señor,' he nodded vigorously. 'Is it dope?' Mahoney asked, and several of the guys including Jesper and Jan looked very interested. 'Marijuana?' I queried and the boy looked puzzled. 'No, señor, *La Bateria, La Bateria*.' He'd now been joined by his young pal and they were both tugging my arms to follow them. Mahoney, Jesper, Jan and I went with them out of the door, followed shortly by George who'd had a quiet word with Enrique. 'He says not to drink or smoke anything they give you, but they won't rob you,' said George, going back inside.

We followed the lads round a couple of corners and ended up at the open door of what looked like a bus shelter. In it was quite an old lady sitting at a table which took up most of the room. '*La Bateria*,' said Juanito proudly. As he spoke the old lady reached under the table and produced with a surprisingly quick and sinewy flourish, a huge battery with leads attached. She spoke rapidly and I couldn't understand a word. It didn't seem to be Spanish and the two lads couldn't tell me exactly what she was saying but the gist of it was that for about a penny she would give us a jolt from this battery, which looked like it was from a big truck or a bulldozer. Jan went to pick it up and looked at the woman with respect. 'Heavy,' he said. Heavy it certainly was and so was this situation getting. She produced what were meant, I think, to be electrodes, which had been cut from a thin piece of sheet metal. She fastened these to the spring clips and put her fingers to her temples meaningfully, then twisted the lead so it made a connection. Nothing happened to the leads but you could see everyone else making the connection. This witch-woman was offering a kind of DIY, Mexican ECT. Forget all your problems for an instant – or maybe forever. Fry your brains for a pittance.

Mahoney gave a grunt of understanding and horror. 'Jesus Christ,' he said 'Naw, *gracias*.' We'd experienced some of this Mexican fascination with electricity the previous night when a couple of clubs we'd been in had electric shock machines, things that you held onto while the waiter ca'ed the handle at the speed you required. A couple of the guys had tried it, but no one tried it twice. Mahoney had been one of the experimenters, but this was not for him. 'Oh my God!' he said, 'let's get these weans out of here.' Jan was also backing away, but Jesper stepped forward. She spat on her fingers and rubbed them on his temples while the boys watched in puzzlement as we tried to stop him. 'It's okay,' he said. She got him to hold the insulated parts of the leads and put the bits of metal on either side of his head. He did so, smiling quietly at our attempts to dissuade him. Mahoney went to take the leads off his head but Jesper said 'No!' with authority and Mahoney stopped. He gave the old lady the nod and she twisted the terminal. At the exact moment she did so Jesper dropped, as Jan later described it 'like someone tackled by Klaus Bergreens'. He went down as though every tendon in his body had been instantaneously severed, and lay twitching with the whites of his eyes showing. Jan uttered some Danish expletive and the old lady stared at Jesper in shock. Jan disconnected the battery as Mahoney and I picked him up. As we did so Jesper turned his head and winked at me where the old lady and the boys couldn't see. We hauled him to his feet with the boys gabbling away in fright and took him out into the sunlight. Jan gave the woman his pocket change and she seemed very grateful.

As soon as we had dragged Jesper round the corner, feet trailing, all very Hollywood, he straightened up and smiled at us. 'I don't think the boys will be trying it, do you?' he said with a smile. Jan was furious with him, cursing away in Danish and stabbing at him with his finger. He explained to us. 'They will come to the Cantina and see Yesper well. This is a foolish thing he has done.' Jesper said that he knew that nothing would happen but he couldn't put forward any convincing reason. He was just sure and he said that he didn't feel anything at all. Jan was still angry with his friend.

We discussed it when we got to La Cantina and the upshot was that Andy, George and Jan went back to *La Bateria* and bought her batteries, of which she had two, for about £5. They brought them back to the pub and Enrique said: 'Put them in the back with the others.' He had about a dozen and he said that when he had enough, 'A truck comes for them.' I asked him where he got them and he smiled and said 'From the mothers.' He also said he'd never tried it but that he believed that it worked on some people but not others. At this everybody turned and stared at Jesper whose face had gone a bit white. 'What kind of country,' he asked, 'has people who want to stop feeling this much?' Enrique said: 'A very poor one, Señor Macho. Is everyone in your country happy, with all your money?' We then pooled most of our cash and sent it to half a dozen addresses that Enrique suggested would be the most needy. We sent it via the young girls who were hanging about outside the bar and he wrote them out receipts to get signed and brought back.

We had a last beer and George called for the bill. At the bottom in big letters it said 'Consejo [which means advice or consultation] $20 Americano', a fair bit of money in Neza. George asked about it and Enrique said 'Free advice is never listened to. The more people are charged for advice, the more they heed it, but you don't need to pay if you don't want to.' We asked what other advice he would give us all and he said 'Listen.

Learn. Do nothing till you understand. And when you do, kill the capitalistas!' He was laughing and so were we. We paid his bill, including the advice, and left on our separate buses, wiser and richer than we had been before we came to Nezahualcoyotl.

11: Snow White and the Godfathers

'Ah *never* get tae be Snow White. How come *ah* never get tae be Snow White?' The Darkie is waxing querulous. Alan Glen is his real name, The Darkie his tribal name, and he is talking about one of our tribal customs. Snow White is a game the Tartan Army plays in foreign cities.

Someone, ideally a brass-necked supercool citizen, goes into a bar on his own, orders a beer, stares at it for a moment or so, takes a sip and throws back his head and shouts in musical style, *à la* Snow White and the Seven Dwarves, 'Hi Ho!' My own experience is that the local punters stare at you for a moment or so, the barman might say something which you don't usually understand anyway and then they pretend nothing has happened. You take another sip, wait for a few seconds and sing it out again. 'Hi Ho!' You have to ignore people saying things to you in Serbo Croat or Norwegian or whatever at this point. You stand and smile down into your beer or into the mirror behind the bar. And you do it again. 'Hi Ho!' Then the door crashes open and the seven dwarves, who've been waiting outside for the third one, march in on their knees and tour the bar singing 'Hi Ho, Hi Ho, it's to the game we go, we'll drink in here, cause it's got good beer. Hi Ho! Hi Ho! Hi Ho!' It helps if you've got some friendly hotel receptionist to give you a phonetic translation of this but even if you haven't, it works anyway. Everybody starts laughing and smiling and the bar is suddenly full of friendly people. Everybody in the world has seen the movie. It has never, ever failed.

The Darkie is still girning 'I can do it, gies a shot.' He has been a pain in the arse since we got to Mexico, muttering about 'Fenians, the lot of them' and 'Lesser breeds without the law'. He has also refused to learn a word of Spanish.

There's a dozen or so of us standing outside our hotel, discussing tactics for the evening ahead. Mahoney catches my eye and winks. George catches on and then Builder John, Anne, The Steelman, Big Andy, Hector Toetector and the rest. There's a couple of guys we've just met, including a retired miner called Digger. They understand also.

'Right, Darkie,' says Mahoney, 'that one over there.'

Mahoney points to a bar a little bit along on the opposite side of the street. It only has a window at one side, and no tables outside, unlike most Mexican bars. We can hide at the side with no windows. We all march over and The Darkie goes in. 'Right,' says The Steelman, 'he's a horrible racist sectarian bastard.'

At that moment The Darkie's first 'Hi Ho' fairly rattles the windows. Andy is peering in, gauging reaction. 'They're talking to him and he's talking back. Wait. Now he's having another glug of his beer.'

'Hi Ho!' This effort is much louder than the first. They have just had a major earthquake here and The Darkie seems intent on creating another one.

'Okay,' says The Steelman 'everybody ready?' We all nod. As The Darkie's third thunderous 'Hi Ho' assaults our ears we all run across the street and round the corner into another bar, laughing and giggling like kids. There are only about four or five other customers so we buy everybody a drink. Builder John is trying to explain what has happened to two young Mexicans and failing. I join in and we finally get it across just as we hear a faint 'Hi Ho' from The Darkie. He is too stupid to give up. Everybody cracks up all over again.

Digger, the retired miner, gives me a nod and we sit at a table. 'You speak Spanish?' he asks. 'A bit.' I am quite proud of my ability with languages but I am not about to boast in this company.

'I need somebody that speaks Spanish,' Digger says, 'I want to adopt a wean.'

He goes on to explain. At the game with Denmark in Nezahualcoyotl two days before, he, like the rest of us, had been appalled by the poverty of its inhabitants. Mile after mile after mile of shacks, mud houses, no sanitation, no electricity, no running water. But the kids were turned out spotlessly. They all had their best clothes on. No shoes sometimes, but their shirts and trousers and skirts were pressed, God knows how, and they smiled at us all the time.

They were genuinely glad to see us. They crowded round in their hundreds asking for autographs. We were like visitors from another planet to them. I asked one of the old men in the street why they kept asking us and the Danes for our autographs. 'You can write, *señor*,' he said.

The Scots and the Danish supporters bought every sweet and chocolate bar in the few tiny hole-in-the-wall shops and gave them in handfuls to the people. A cheap gesture in cash terms. A whole shelf only cost me and George about £3. But the Neza people appreciated it.

Many of them had been given tickets by the Mexican government, presumably as a sop for siting a multi-billion peso soccer paradise in the midst of mind-numbing and soul-grinding desolation, and some tried to give their tickets to us. Not sell them to us – though the face value was about two weeks wages for them. The Danes and us paid full whack. You would have too if you had been there.

A Kilwinning father and son were negotiating with a wee lad of about nine or ten. They needed two tickets and he only had one. He gave them his ticket, without asking for the money, said 'Wait' and returned about five minutes later with another boy who had a ticket. He also handed it over. Jim and James, the Kilwinningites, had a job getting them to take face value. I saw the kids looking after them pityingly as they left.

Something like the above had happened to Digger and he was intent on repaying honesty and faith.

'Listen, Wee Man, I've been scrapped as a worker, but I can still do something. I got nearly 20 grand redundo from the pit. I've spoken to the wife and she's keen as mustard.'

Digger looks about 60. Builder John says 'But you'll be dead before the wean grows up.' John's wife Anne is shushing him but he's trying to make a point. 'That wouldn't be fair to the kid, growing up in a foreign country.'

'No sir,' says Digger, 'my mother and father both lived well into their 80s and anyway I've already got three sons and a daughter, all married. I've got five grandweans. He'll be well looked after if anything happens to us. He'll be family.'

'He?' Anne is quick.

'Well, Meg and me aren't sure. I think a boy would be better. He could fight if there were problems. He could play fitba. What do you think?'

The argument and discussion raged into the night and got more grandiose as the night wore on and the bottles went down. By about midnight we had his house built by John, wired by Bodyswerve, George has coached him to a degree at Edinburgh University.

Mahoney is indignant, Glaswegian pride insulted. 'Edinburgh, what has it got? A castle, a smile and a song. Wan out of three isny bad.'

George is equally defensive of his home. 'Funny how all the Wise Men are from the East and all the cowboys from the West.'

Anne and Digger have been discussing practicalities. A list of things to do has been drawn up.

One of the young Mexican guys we'd been talking to earlier has joined in the discussion. His name is Ramon and he is a trade union organiser. He looks at us all measuringly. 'You will do this?' He shouted something at the barman and left. The barman brought us drinks which Ramon had paid for and the plans continued. Andy will teach the kid snooker. Mahoney will help him fiddle his taxes. I will get him a job.

Ramon came back in with a tall quiet man whom he introduced as the union's lawyer, who speaks excellent English and has been to Aberdeen. He speaks soberly and at length with Digger and Anne, shakes hands all round and leaves.

Next morning George, John, Anne and I went with Digger to the lawyer's office. You need a certificate from a psychiatrist saying you are sane to adopt a child in Mexico. Digger still has it, framed on his wall.

And the boy is here. I won't tell you his name, and I lied about Meg's and Digger's names. But Andy is teaching him snooker and when he's old enough we'll do the best we can with our own boasts. He might be our secret weapon in the World Cup 2002!

12: The Siegfried Kirschen Fan Club

It's a strange place, Cyprus, full of heavily armed Greeks and equally heavily armed and totally paranoid Turks staring with hate at each other across barbed wire and fortifications that would put the Maginot Line to shame, and which are just as useless as that turned out to be.

Despite this, both lots are very pleasant people to strangers, it's just each other that they hate: and the British Army: and the UN, who annoy the shit out of both sides by refusing to let them kill each other.

Mahoney served in Cyprus with the British Army and as an emissary from the Tartan Army, he had been sent ahead to make smooth a place for us, his first assignment from our squad, and one that he wanted to carry out with honour. He was not happy when he met us at the airport, a military one full of very scary people.

He wasn't scary but scared. 'There's going to be bother,' he said, 'I can feel it in my water. The guys from the British Army are looking to cause trouble with the locals and they're going to use the game as a focus.'

We set off to one of Scotball's hotels to see if we could find

Uncle Ken, their security and crowd control man. He was in the hotel but nobody could find him and while we were all sitting in the bar waiting for him we were joined by about 20 guys in the full fig – new kilts, new socks, bonnets, feathers, plaids, Saltires, Lion Rampants, the lot. We only usually get dressed up like this for the games, and we travel in Scotland top and kilt or trousers, but these guys were intent on creating the whole Mongol/Vandal barbarian horde image, though the highly polished shoes gave most of them away as new boys.

Builder John is the longest-serving in our squad, starting during the qualification for Germany, and he was regaling them with German stories, with most of these young and not-so-young lads hanging on every word.

'Do you remember that autobahn café, and the squad from Glasgow?' Anne started to laugh. 'And Big Mac the Chef,' she prompted. 'Tell them about Big Mac.'

Said John: 'We had stopped the van for a break at this big café on the road to Dortmund for the Zaire game when a busload of the hairiest-arsed desperados you ever saw came strolling in. They all worked, or had worked for Stakis and other Glasgow hotels, and they'd pooled their money and hired this clapped-out bus – or maybe they bought it. A tenner would have been too much. Somebody had a hippy background because the destination board just said "Forward". Anyway, there were two or three Teutonic busloads in front of them, standing in a neat queue, at least until they got to the food, when they all started pushing and shouting at the people serving them. It was obviously going to be a long wait before they got served. Big Mac came over and sat beside us. He was about 5ft 5in and roly-poly, nearly round, which is why, he told us, he was called Big Mac. He was round with plenty of fat and a really quick cooker, he said. He wasn't happy with the wait, particularly as the place didn't sell booze, and he had a word with three or four of his guys in the queue, who then beetled off into the bog. I didn't see them coming back out,' but Anne did, and it was five minutes before I noticed anything. In fact I didn't really see anything going on until a big guy with a T-shirt that said "Scotland the Wee" came out from behind the food counter with two plates and plonked them down in front of Big Mac and his mate. Black pudding, bacon, eggs – even fried bread, that black chewy stuff you get there – they'd deep fried it.'

'Aye, there were half a dozen of them back there, busy cooking up everything that was lying about,' said Anne. 'The people behind the counter were that astonished that they never said a word, but the Germans in the queue were outraged, at least until the guys started cooking to order for them. There were only three or four staff on, and the guys just set up a relay system once their mates had got theirs. The staff would tell them what to cook and they just did it for about half an hour. They even took the plates of food out to the Germans – it was supposed to be service at the counter – and took money back to the cashier. They even got tips.'

John took up the tale again, 'Big Mac had finished and he was looking around, smiling a bit. "You'll notice," he said to me "that their hands are clean and their hair is off their faces."

'I hadn't, to be honest,' said John, 'I was too busy looking at the two foot long hair, ditto beard and the tartan boiler suit that one guy was wearing over a filthy dress shirt with a bow tie that looked like a fried butterfly.'

'Be fair,' said Anne, 'he wasn't serving and as I recall, you tried to get me to make you one of those boiler suits when we got home.' John fell silent and Anne went on, 'Big Mac told us that they'd never done it before and that they hadn't planned anything, it was just done on the spur of the moment. But the best bit was the Germans singing "For He's a Jolly Good Fellow", in English. They banged their glasses and knives and forks on the table like "For He's a Jolly Good Fellow" – Crash! "For He's a" – and so on. I don't know who started it but it went on for ages with Big Mac taking bows and waving the rest of his boys onto their feet to take their own bows. I've never seen Germans do anything as spontaneous as that before or since. It was like being in that beer hall in Munich – the Hofbrauhaus – but without the organised singing and chanting.'

John spoke again. 'Big Mac paying was great too. He had the kitty and he went up to the cashier, who sent him back to our table and went for the manager. Lots of the Germans spoke to him as he arrived and he was smiling when he approached the table. "How many?" he asked. "Thirty seven" was the reply. "Two hundred marks and thank you, but please do not do this in our restaurant again!".'

John and Anne were smiling at each other as they reminisced and so were the listeners. 'He was a good guy, that manager. He could take a joke and he charged them less than a pound a head. Big Mac was well pleased. He paid up and they all went and shook hands with the staff, who were still working away serving the people coming in, though there were no queues. You don't get many like him or like that manager. You don't get many Germans with a sense of humour.' John disagreed, 'Remember Siggy – yon boy was funny.' Anne said, 'Oh aye, Siggy, what a black dirty laugh.' And they laughed quietly together while we all waited for them to go on.

Just then a young bloke came bustling into the bar. 'Couple of the lads in a wee bit of bother with the authorities,' he said a bit breathlessly, 'anyone here know a lawyer?' Five out of the 20 odd were actually lawyers and George and I were talking about what makes these sensible, middle-class careerists dress up like refugees from Culloden when Mahoney interrupted, 'You're a fucking uni professor or something and you're the managing director of a big employment agency. What are you talking about? I'm the slum scumbag here.'

'Me and the Wee Man here both had outside toilets when we were wee. I was ten before I moved to a house with a bath and that was only because my father got a job as a janny at the Masonic Hall,' said George, 'so shut yer geggie.' George has worked so hard at making his speech precise and ironing out his Edinburgh schemie accent that when he tried to do the patois he sounded ridiculous, and we all fell about.

'Hello,' said one of the erstwhile lawyers, 'Alasdair with a "d" is the name, but you can call me Alastair with a "t", everybody does.' He was immediately dubbed 'Alastair with a "d", by George and he joined the company, shaking hands around and reversing his grip, Harlem style, in what some winder-upper had told him was the international recognition sign of the Tartan Army. His next words, though, immediately qualified him as a potential recruit because he said eagerly, 'Do you know that you can get to Beirut really easily from here?' Mahoney was staring at him in astonished horror. 'Befuckingruit, is it, ya daft big bastard. For why would you want to go there, for Christ's sake? If you want to get shot just go downtown into Limassol and shout "Turkey is great". Somebody will oblige.'

Alastair with a 'd' was a bit taken aback by Mahoney's vehemence. He said, 'Well, I thought if a lot of us went we could sort of move around in a group, a phalanx, kind of.' Mahoney the military expert was amused. 'A phalanx was a solid unit of heavily armed and armoured Greek infantry, but the ancient Greeks didn't know fuck all about machine guns or rifles, did they? That's why phalanxes are a bit thin on the ground, these days.' And he was off to the happy hour bar muttering 'Fucking phalanxes, is it?' but he was back in a minute with a drink for Al D, as he became. He's a decent big spud from the Borders who has since moved to Glasgow and the fact that he is still alive and unkidnapped is entirely down to Mahoney, who spent the next ten minutes outlining in precise detail why Al D shouldn't go to Beirut, despite its proximity.

'Could we not just sort of go and hang about the docks and get the next boat back, just to say we've been?' asked Al D plaintively. Mahoney looked around at all of us for help. 'Where do all the thieves, toe rags and riff raff gather in every port? Where?' and we all chorused: 'The docks.' Al D said, 'But could we not kind of hide, like?' He was wearing a Stewart tartan kilt, white socks with tabs and a skean dhu, which he had smuggled in his suitcase, because they won't let you wear them on the plane. He had on a white shirt with a Lion Rampant over his shoulder and a giant bunnet with a red toorie and a huge peacock feather sticking out of it. All he needed was a beer in his hand and a slightly less sheepish look to be the perfect footsoldier. 'Hide!' Mahoney's voice was a screech 'Fuckin hide! What are you going to hide behind? Maybe one of the giant pink elephants that infest the wharves of Beruit or the cut-outs of Tartan Army punters that they put up for target practice? Form yourself into a phalanx and march over to the bar and get me a beer, ya eejit.'

By this time word had came through that there were two guys in the nick but that they were getting out. When they eventually arrived, having stumped up £200 bail with a court date months ahead and no chance of getting it back, they were angry. What had happened was that two women had joined them at their table and in the manner of their kind all over the world, had ordered champagne. 'Two hundred and fifty quid for a bottle of champagne?' said Wee Alex, the smaller of the two. 'And it wasn't even French. Alex here told them where to go and when they started getting stroppy he went and got one of the Cypriot guys in the bar to phone the police. When they got there they tried to make us pay the bill and when we wouldn't they arrested us. We went quietly. Have you seen the guns and batons they've got? When they got us to the station they took everything off us and when we got it back we were 250 quid short, and we still had to pay the bail!' Peter, one of the lawyers who'd gone to rescue them, cocked a sardonic eye. 'I'm pretty sure it's a scam with the police and the restaurant owners. I've been to see them and they say they didn't get any money from the police, but they also said they would drop the charges if the police allowed them to. I'm sure they got half the money. They were smirking like they'd got one over us. There doesn't seem to be anything that we can do. It's the system.'

'I'll fix their system for them,' said Wee Alex. And he did. With the help of a couple of guys in the bar and Loucas the barman, the following day he had 1,000 cheap leaflets printed with the name of the bar and what had happened. The lawyers wouldn't let him put anything about who had the money but the story itself put you off going there, as it was intended to. Alex and Wee Alex went round all the Tartan Army hotels and pubs with the leaflets that day, and as far as I know nobody went near the place for the whole week we were there. It must have cost the place a fortune, which they would have earned even without the scam, as the Limassol pubs did a roaring trade. They also both went down at lunchtime to the bar that had robbed them and stood across the road, shouting Scots across as they went to go in and giving them leaflets. 'Wee Alex was charging them a fiver a time for the advice,' said Alex. 'That's right,' said Wee Alex, 'we made 25 quid and that paid for the leaflets and a few Keos, but nobody will let us buy a drink. We might even end up showing a profit on the trip if we don't have to buy booze.'

Keo is the name of the local beer and the words of the then current advert for Trio biscuits, which had a wee cartoon girl loudly demanding Trio, were cannibalised and you could hear it coming out of every pub on the island 'Keo, Ke-e-eo! I want a Keo and I want one now.' Keo also make brandy. Not very good brandy, but the local drink is a brandy sour, which disguises the fact that it has got more hangover-producing stuff in it than a crate of port and a barrel of red wine. I started drinking them in a bar across from the Elias Beach Hotel, where Mahoney and a couple of the others had gone to consult Uncle Ken on security, because I met a couple of old Cypriot guys who were telling me the history of Cyprus in excellent English and they were drinking them.

I woke up at noon the next day with George shaking me and with the worst hangover I have ever had in my entire life. Umpteen Alka Seltzers, showers and bottles of tonic water later I was lying moaning wee moans to myself while George filled me in. 'You bought everyone in the place a brandy sour and then you drank the ones of the people who didn't want them. Then you tried to buy the bar and when that didn't work you started trying to give people money. I took it off you and I've got it here in my pocket. They also gave you a bottle of brandy to take away and I've got it in my room. I didn't think you'd want any at the moment. Then you were in the fountain at the front of the hotel. That was before you tried to get the lovely Marjory to come to your room by swearing that you had Sean Connery up there. Okay, I lied about the lovely Marjory, that was me, but it was your fault. You told the Steelman that you had big Sean staying with you and he convinced everybody else.'

I spent the rest of the day skulking in the sauna and the pool, trying to stop my hands shaking and hoping that the wee blue flashes at the edge of my vision would go away. When I finally got my act together at about eight o'clock and went down to get something to eat, the entire dining room, including about 50 Germans, clapped and cheered when I entered.

George and the Steelman and several others shouted me over to join them and George said, 'They're just trying to thank you for sponsoring the pool competition. The Wee Man's One Grand Challenge, we've decided to call it.' They told me that I had been in the snooker room last night insisting that I could beat anybody and they told me that I had put up £1,000 for a knockout competition to be held that very evening. I was attempting to demur, but I felt so ill that I found it difficult to argue. The Steelman said, 'You're always saying to us if you can't do the time, don't do the crime, so you've got to do it.' I don't recall saying this to the Steelman or to anyone else, ever, but he is so persuasive that I just nodded, though I had no idea where I was going to find £1,000, or for that matter, if I did, how I was going to account for it to my wife, joint custodian of the family fortunes.

After dinner we all went into the pool room where there were four tables that the management had held for us, making some of the Germans unhappy, until George invited them to join the tourney. Now I didn't mind one of the Army, and particularly our squad, winning my money, as it would be redistributed in the pubs and restaurants, and 'it is no loss what a freen gets' as the saying has it, but I was buggered if I was going to let some anonymous sauerkraut swallower make off with my dosh. The tourney was organised so that I played the winner for the £1,000, and it soon became clear that I would be playing either Big Andy, who is far and away our best player, or this German guy called Klaus. I got more and more nervous as the final approached, but it was over almost in a flash, with Andy poised to pot the black ball to win. He did, but the cue ball followed through, an unimaginable lapse by Andy, and it was down to me and Klaus, or Barbie as George had started calling him.

I'm not the best player in the world but I am very lucky, because I play to crowd my luck and I expect good things to happen. This was one of those games where I got extremely lucky, with all my lot going 'Wee Man! Wee Man!' and all the Germans going 'Klaus-e! Klaus-e!' whenever we did something good. I was shaking like a leaf, trying to concentrate, playing slowly, and Klaus was strolling round casually banging them in as if tomorrow belonged to him. It came down to a black ball game as well with, unbelievably, Klaus doing exactly the same as Andy, so I won, and my money was safe. My legs were shaking so much that I had to sit down, and George got the drinks in for me. I was pretty chuffed with myself but managed to refrain from bumming about it, for which I'm glad, as they told me the next morning that it had all been a set-up. I hadn't promised to put up the money and the whole tourney had been fixed so that I had to play Klaus, who was a semi-pro. He'd been in on it, and had cleverly thrown the game. I played him later for a pound and only managed to pot one ball. 'The biter bit. The biter bit,' said the extremely gleeful Bodyswerve, and *schadenfreude*, the dark pleasure in the misfortunes of others for which only the Germans have a word, was rife in that room, adding a wee tang to my honey and yoghurt breakfast.

I didn't drink anything for two days after that experience and I haven't been able to look a brandy sour in the glass since, but it was a salutary lesson. Not to not drink, but to carefully examine any statements about me made by my comrades in arms. I got a bit of admiration as well from the Germans, as Klaus said. 'You would have paid the money, yes?' and George and Andy said 'Aye,' before I could open my mouth. They had trusted him not to win and he was a good young guy who also told jokes and stories with humour as black as three yards up a chimney at midnight.

This indirectly led to John and Anne telling their Siggy story after dinner that night. We'd been up to the Turkish part with Klaus and a few of the others and there was a kind of anti-militarism feeling going on. The Germans were on holiday from some kind of college and they were all about 20 and up for a lark – and pleasant with it as well. No side at all to them. Klaus had told some sort of anti-authoritarian joke and Anne said, 'That reminds me of Siggy.' None of us had heard of Siggy at that time, though he's become a talking point since, and Builder John and Anne have told it several times.

'We were down in Munich to see one of John's National Service pals who had married a German lass and moved there. He took us out to the Hofbrauhaus place, a really huge pub with women carrying a dozen of these big steins of beer at a time.' John interrupted, 'It's really strong beer as well. I gargled down three steins and then it occurred to me that I had just drunk three litres in about half an hour.'

'It occurred to him when he fell onto his hands and knees when he got up to go to the loo, and his pal David wasn't much better, though he should have known better,' said Anne. 'We were all right after a wee walk about,' said John. 'Tommy showed me a special room in the bog for being sick in. Its called the *krankenhaus* or something like that. Organised, eh! I wasn't feeling sick, just giggly, but that's looking ahead, isn't it?'

There was a short pause while we contemplated a culture unafraid to stare that particularly unpleasant aspect of the effect of alcohol in the face and to plan for it. 'The Monster should move there,' said the Steelman, as Mac the piper was downtown picking the people who were going to have to carry him home groaning later on that night.

'Anyway,' continued John, 'when Davie and I got back from the bog Anne and Davie's wife Marti were being chatted up by this Latin smoothie.'

'He'd been selling flowers in the bar and had just sold his last one,' said Anne, only to be interrupted yet again by John who said, 'buying roses in ones in a bar is God's way of telling you that you have far too much money.'

'His name was Max and he was not a happy chappy,' said Anne. 'He'd never been in Munich before and he'd been living somewhere in Sweden, though he looked like a Turk or an Armenian or something. What he wanted was someone to take him to Dachau, to the concentration camp. It's just a couple of miles north of Munich and Marti and David knew where it was. The train to it takes about 15 minutes. The thing was that he didn't want to go on his own. He seemed like a nice enough guy, even if he was a wee bit strange, so the four of us said we'd go with him the next morning. He was a gypsy and some of his family had been taken there and killed.'

'We know Dachau and the others,' said Klaus, who had given George a serious talking to when someone had told him that Klaus Barbie was a Nazi butcher. 'The Nazis killed many *Zigeunerin*, many gypsies. It is difficult to understand for me and for my friends. We are taught about it in school, but my parents do not wish to talk of these times because their parents, my grandparents, will not talk to them of it at all. My father was born in 1945 and he and his family had hard times after the war.' Bodyswerve said, with one of those bursts of insight that occasionally lance the boil, 'It must be really shite being a young German.'

'Yes, yes,' said Klaus, 'people do not like us even before they meet us and it is not our fault, it is the fault of the people of my grandparents age, and they mostly are dead. They are guilty, we are not, and they will not talk of their guilt.'

'Can I finish this story?' asked John testily, and went on 'the four of us met Max the next morning at the Hauptbahnhof where the train to Dachau leaves from, and he was pretty freaky. He was as nervous as anything when we joined the queue and he was rattling away to Marti in German. It was quite a long queue and by the time we got to the ticket window he was totally gibbering. The young guy on the ticket desk – he couldn't have been much older than Klaus here – was the final straw for Max. He had short blond hair in a crew cut, thin lips, pale blue eyes, rimless glasses, wee thin tie, perfect shirt. All he needed was a swastika on his collar to be the archetypal Nazi in every movie you've ever seen. The young guy asked what we wanted and Max suddenly started shouting at him. Marti and David were translating what he was saying, and he was demanding free tickets to Dachau, like they gave his father and his cousins and uncles. He went on for ages. It was really embarrassing.

'The young guy wasn't feart. He asked, "You wish returns?" without the glimmer of a smile, and Marti was dead shocked. The rest of the queue was listening avidly and there was a serious hiss as this got passed back. Then he said, in German of course, "I understand. You wish five returns to Dachau. Okay. I will pay for them. You don't pay. I will pay!" Marti and the queue were pretty pleased about this and there was a smug hum from them. Then he leaned forward and said quite loudly, "Please put your gold teeth and your spectacles in the basket over there." And the thing is, everybody, including Max turned and looked to where he was pointing. I'd no idea what he had said but when Marti told us I just started to laugh. It's the blackest thing I have ever heard anyone say and I thought it was totally hilarious. So did Siggy, which was his name, we found out later, because I could see a grin tugging away at the corners of his mouth.'

Anne said, 'You just had to laugh. Marti was standing there totally gobsmacked and John and Dave had their arms round Max's shoulders and they were both tee-heeing away like weans, but trying to jolly him up as well. And Siggy was red in the face with trying not to laugh. The queue just evaporated and once Marti and David had taken Max away we invited Siggy out for a beer and we ended up buying him lunch when he got his break. What a laugh he was. I wish we'd kept in touch with him but I don't even know his second name. He was called Siegfried, Siggy for short and he was funnier than any of these stand-up comedians. He told stories like Billy Connolly except about German people and their stupidities and his English was perfect.'

'He spoke Italian, Spanish and French as well, and he was learning Russian, he told us,' said John. 'He said in all seriousness that he just wanted to live long enough to bring down the Berlin Wall.'

Klaus had been laughing at Siggy's sick joke on Max, unlike most of his friends who looked as shocked as Anne said Marti did, but he got serious when the Wall was mentioned. 'We, not these friends here,' he said, gesturing behind him, 'but other friends and I, we will pull down *Die Mauer*. I am from Berlin and we talk to friends in the East every day. Next year – maybe the one after that. But it will come down. We can do that for Siggy, for ourselves and for all of Germany.'

This was in February of 1989, and he got his prediction wrong, as the Wall was smashed in November of that year, by Klaus and many others. He sent me a picture of him shaking hands with his friends across it, and later he sent me some tiny pieces of it, which I still have.

The next day we went to the mountains and threw snowballs at each other. We even built a wall for Klaus to storm through, which he did, screaming like a mad banshee. When we got back there was a wedding going on in the hotel. George and I gatecrashed it and soon all the Scots were invited. As George said, 'If there is dancing on the tables to be done, we are the boys to do it.' And there was, later on, after I had done some dancing of my own.

The bride's father and her uncles had been doing that Zorba the Greek dance thing, dancing in lines with their arms over each other's shoulders. I'm not a great dancer but I fancied I could do it. At this particular time I was the proud possessor of a very long ponytail, grown especially to freak out staid business people at my place of work. I was the boss so nobody could tell me off. That evening I'd brushed it out, sending messages in Cypriot of which I was blissfully unaware. A guy came over and indicated that he wanted to dance and I, much encouraged by the others, accepted. As I stood up I was whisked into his arms and off at speed around the floor while he breathed what I assume were endearments and blandishments into my ear. I managed to extricate myself after a few seconds, but not without a small struggle, and I returned to our table as the group sang the now traditional 'You'll like Jimmy Hill'. This song, incidentally, is now on the Net in its original version in 18 languages, with more being added all the time. You can access it at *sadbastardsrus* UK, should you so desire.

That incident led to brief exposure in the *Glasgow Herald* diary, as the diarist was present, laughing hugely at my discomfort, but he listened to my pleas and preserved my anonymity, he claimed, by just calling me 'the Wee Man from Maryhill', which is what all of the Army call me, so only they, and then everyone else in the world, knew I'd been dancing with a bloke. Some anonymity.

Also anonymous, until this moment, were the people who took the towels off the German guests at another big hotel. Some of the Army had been telling us that there was a big bunch of Bavarian bampots doing their usual stuff, pushing to the front of queues, hogging the recliners at the pool, that sort of thing. Klaus and a couple of his pals had heard about this, had gone to talk with them and returned very angry. Next day he woke George and me at 8 a.m. and took us along the road to the hotel and then up to the roof, laughing and looking like they'd done something daring. Apparently the Germans in the hotel employed one of their number to go down to the pool at 6 a.m. and put towels on every available seat, so that only Germans could sit there. Klaus and his pals had been up early doors and had taken the towels and arranged them creatively on the beach – in the shape of a swastika, a giant white and stripy swastika. 'That, I think, will send them the message,' said Klaus, 'that their behaviour is not right.' George asked, 'But won't they think that you are a Nazi?' and Klaus said 'They know we are not Nazis. This is telling them what we think they are. But we do not wish them to know that it was us. There are no jokes about swastikas made at home, not ever.'

So George and I claimed it and got bought gallons of drinks by the people who were staying in the hotel. George and Klaus took photos from the roof and they were passed from hand to hand for days.

When the day of the game finally arrived we were all on tenterhooks, because Mahoney had been right about the organised violence. There were English thugs in the pubs threatening to turn up in Scotland jerseys and one really horrible bastard had had his forcibly removed by a bunch of Border lads, including Al D, who told us about it. 'We tried to get his head off as well,' he said, 'but it was fixed on pretty tight. Not as tight as it was before we started, but pretty tight. His mates just sat and left us to it, so there might not be as much trouble as Tom Mahoney thinks.'

And there wasn't, at least not from the British Army guys, though there were a few of them there, shouting insults at the Cypriots. During the game, which was a disgrace to the name of football, we were surrounded by huge walls of barbed wire with a moat at the front, and nobody could get near us. The Cypriot team started falling down right away, and the ref seemed to be taking it seriously, speaking to the Scottish players with severity and wagging his finger at them. Anne said: 'Hey John, is that not Siggy from Munich?' John didn't think so, but when at one point he got near the touchline Anne shouted 'Hello Siggy!' and he looked up, but he had no idea who had shouted.

At full time it was still two each and the Cypriot players were driving everyone crazy. Sometimes they fell down when no one was within ten yards of them. It was appalling. People behind us were singing the Drawing Song, 'Egypt, Iran, Ireland too, we've drawn with them and we'll draw with you'. As a bunch of folk I didn't know started to leave I said 'Don't go, you'll miss the goal,' and they stayed, as I swore we'd score. The tension was terrible as the extra time stretched and stretched. The Steelman had his stopwatch out and he was going 'eight minutes 30 seconds, eight minutes 40 seconds', when Richard Gough went up and headed it in. The place went totally mental as the ref blew for time up, especially the Cypriot fans, some of whom attacked us as we left. 'Always move slowly towards the polis if there's trouble,' said the Steelman. 'Not these fucking polis I'm not,' said Mahoney, as we edged our way to safety while trying to protect ourselves from the kicks and punches, and he was right, because they were making no moves of any kind to stop the group attempting to hit us, and a few of them were fingering their clubs and looking at us in a very upsetting way.

We eventually all squeezed into a tiny café while the Cypriots were totally trashing the official bus, throwing big blocks of stones through the windows and trying to set it on fire. They were banned by FIFA for this behaviour, and they deserved it. 'They got caught in their own cheating trap,' said Anne. 'I can't stand cheats or sore losers. Did you notice them trying to get at Siggy when he was running off? It is him, you know, I swear he winked at me during the game.' John was laughing. 'A nice fantasy, darlin.'

Mahoney was keeping lookout on the door and he snagged Al D and some of his pals as they were going past. 'Do you know how we got out?' he asked Mahoney, then answered himself with delight. 'We formed a phalanx and just forced our way through them. We did it, we formed a phalanx.' Al D had a programme with him and we looked up the referee to see who had been our saviour. Siegfried Kirschen is his name, and we instantly formed the Siegfried Kirschen Nine and Half Minutes Fan Club, Tartan Army Branch. I'm the treasurer and there are a few bob in the kitty towards a bottle of his favourite tipple should our paths cross, as I hope they do, because he was an honest and fair man, doing a good job in impossible and threatening circumstances. He was East German and we started a nasty rumour about him that night, just to annoy the Cypriots, and it did, because all the Cypriots that we told it too instantly believed it, which gives you an insight into their ideas of honesty and fairness. It's a question: 'What's the difference between an East German referee and a West German referee?' to which the answer is 'East German referees are cheaper'.

I apologise to Herr Kirschen for this, as George and I thought it up, but we got a fair amount of mileage out of it and we understand *schadenfreude* a bit better as well. The song that night was 'If you knew Siggy, Like we know Siggy, Oh, Oh, Oh what a pal. You give him money, his watch goes funny, until we score the winning goal.' It annoyed the shit out of the Cypriots and it rubbed their noses in the fact that it was their own cheating and lying down that added on the extra time.

Anne still swears it was her Siggy and she even wrote to him via FIFA but she didn't get a reply. 'He might reply yet,' said John, 'time means different things to different people.' And it does to us, which is why 'I'll see you down the pub in ten minutes', is now 'see you down the pub in a Siggy'.

13: Pistols and Pescatores

The Tartan Army word for 'shush!' or 'quiet!' is *pescatores*! It started in a beautiful wee place called Sestri Levante, which is about 20 minutes up the coast from Genoa. It's a long story.

We had watched our doughty warriors crumble to the might of Costa Rica that night, the fourth time out of seven that we'd lost an opening game in the World Cup finals. Genoa was a miserable place, with about 10,000 of the Army walking about looking for beer. The Italians had imposed a 24 hour alcohol ban and although many of the lads and lasses had taken the precaution of stocking up, almost as many hadn't, and you could hear shouts of 'Anybody in a pub that's selling booze?' and 'Anybody got any drink?' all over town.

We were doubly blessed and very secure on the oblivion front, as we had already established that a reasonable-sized hostelry round the corner and down hundreds of steps from the station would be welcoming us. We had offered the *patron* money but he had declined, saying that he disagreed with the ban and that he would stay open for as long as we wanted to be served. 'It's not as if you are *Inglesi*,' he said.

The other plank of our drinking-to-forget platform was in Special K's minibus, as he had brought about two dozen cases of

117

Tennent's lager all the way from London, though where he got them in London I've no idea. We each armed ourselves with six cans (a bargain at £5) and set off to bring succour to our countrymen and women and also to gift some genuine Scottish beer to any Costa Rican fans we could find. They were a bit thin on the ground but as we were making our miserable way up towards the big square with the fountain in the middle, the Piazza de Ferrari, Mahoney and a new recruit, The Heart, shouted 'Hallo!' and took off at speed to greet two expensively dressed citizens in Costa Rican hats. These two gentlemen, seeing them approach, very sensibly took to their heels and fled up a side street, only to find another Army phalanx, this one with a piper at its head, filling the narrow alley. They then chose us as the least risk option as there were only about a dozen of us, and turned round with their arms open saying '*Por favor, senors*'.

Once we'd established that the giving of lager was our aim and not the mayhem they had expected, they were extremely affable. They told us their names, which everybody instantly forgot, as they were both long and liquid streams of syllables, so we just called them Costa and Rica, which amused them no end. They called all of us 'Scotland', except they say it 'Ehscotland'. They made an exception for the two women with us. They called them 'Ehsignorina Ehscotland', a combination of Italian and Spanish that made Anne laugh every time one or other of them said it. They asked if they could come with us and we fell upon them with friendship. They were also good for not frightening the other three Costa Ricans that we met on the way to the square. One of them was an astonishingly good looking woman of about 20 and The Heart was instantly smitten. In about five seconds he had his arm round her waist and was chatting away volubly. He was talking the biggest plate of mince I have ever heard, all about him being a big number in computers and how he was glad we were going to Ferrari Square because it reminded him of his car at home, which was parked with the Rolls-Royce in front of his castle in his ancestral grounds. She was nodding away quite the thing, as she hadn't a clue what he was saying, but she obviously enjoyed the attention and she didn't seem to mind the arm round the waist. I had a word with Luis, one of the group she was with, as the Latin folk we'd met round the world seem a trifle more protective of their womenfolk than most, but he said it was okay, she was her own woman. He was understanding about a tenth of The Heart's patter and he asked me if any of it was true. I'd only just met The Heart, who'd joined up with our lot the day before while Special K and I were barrelling our way through France and Switzerland at 110 miles per hour. Special K is a driver and a half and he got us to the game with 15 minutes to spare after we got held up by Customs, which isn't supposed to exist, for four hours, but that's another story. I was on what is the driver's side in Italy and Special K kept passing Italians by a thousandth of an inch or so. You'd need to have seen Italian drivers to realise what a feat that phrase actually encompasses and after the twentieth or thirtieth near miss I just shut my eyes and hoped that my death wouldn't be painful.

The Heart had come up to George and Big Andy and a few of the others the previous day and simply said, 'Is it all right if I join you? I'm a bit lonely, my name's Hunter.' George said, 'Ah, The Heart Is a Lonely Hunter,' a movie from the '60s, he told me, with Alan Arkin as a lonely deaf mute. He can tell you the name of every movie ever made, plus the plot and who starred in it. 'Only the ones in English,' he says. That's how The Heart got his name and he quite likes it. 'As long as it's not The Hib,' he had said to George. The Heart supports Cowdenbeath, God help him, which is probably why he was lonely.

I told Luis that I doubted if any of the bumming was true and he explained that The Heart had a big surprise coming, as Angelina, or to be more accurate, Angelina's parents, had great gobbets of dough and that she was in fact used to people with Ferraris and Rolls-Royces. Both Luis and Ramon worked for her parents and they were keeping an eye on her while the World Cup was on and then afterwards on her trip round Europe. George asked if Cowdenbeath was on her itinerary and Luis said 'If it is not a major capital, no, I do not think so.'

Costa and Rica knew who Angelina was and they told George and me something we should have deduced about Luis and Ramon, '*Guardia*', they said, tapping the inside pockets of their jackets, 'bodyguards'. As George and I were debating whether to inform the rest of the company that we were now accompanied by two men who were probably armed, and an heiress wearing clothing that could have not concealed an aspirin, we arrived in the Square. There was some desultory splashing and Angelina was sitting very prettily on the edge of the fountain, giggling. She really is a stunning looking girl and if her bodyguards weren't being overly possessive then The Heart was making up for them. He was glued to her side, shooting dark looks and fiery glances at anyone who came within ten feet of them. He asked Angelina, who spoke some English but had a bit of difficulty with his accent, as does everyone else, if she would like to come to dinner with him. He had somewhere acquired a long-stemmed carnation which he'd given to her. Unlike most women of my acquaintance, she knew how to deal with a flower. She didn't discard it immediately, as some of them do, and she didn't hold it awkwardly, but passed it from hand to hand, laying it on her cheek etc., with grace and elegance. The Heart was totally smitten and if his tongue had been hanging out any further he would have tripped over it. She was a flirt and she was bloody good at it. She probably went to a school to learn it.

There wasn't much happening in the Square, so we decided that we would go to a restaurant, even if they didn't serve us wine. Luis recommended one so we all trooped round to it, to find Mahoney and Big Andy shaking their heads in front of the menu outside. 'It'll cost us about 50 quid each to get out of here,' said Andy. 'I'd rather have a pizza.'

Angelina didn't understand the problem and wanted to go in which meant that The Heart had to go in, which meant that Luis and Ramon were going in too. They did and about ten seconds later while we were talking about what to do and where to go The Heart re-emerged 'I've only got about 50 quid on me,' he said 'anybody good for a tap?' George was trying to tell him that it might be a good idea to let Angelina treat him, but he was outraged. 'No woman is paying for me,' he muttered. 'But it's okay if we do it?' asked Anne. 'She doesn't even have a purse or a handbag with her,' The Heart said with finality, 'so I'm paying. I'll pay you back.' We scrounged up some money, which was relatively easy, as it was early on in the trip. George and Special K were trying to explain to him who Ramon and Luis were but he thought we were sending him up because we had overheard the outrageous lies he'd been telling her. 'All's fair in love and Italy,' he said. 'This is where Romeo and Juliet shagged.' George was instantly apoplectic. 'Shagged! Shagged! You soulless lout, that was in Verona and they didn't shag, as you put it.' 'That's what they told their parents and Shakespeare,' said The Heart, who was a lonely Hunter no longer, as he nipped back into the restaurant.

We decided to go to our pub, picking up carry-out food on the way and by the time we got there we had acquired another half dozen Scots. Costa and Rica were still with us and we met The Darkie with another couple of Costa Rican fans just as we arrived. The *patron* welcomed us, though we were a bit disconcerted to see that, of the dozen or so customers in the bar, about half were police; off duty, but still in their fancy uniforms. We were told that everything was okay and that the local police headquarters was just around the corner, so there would be no trouble. I still find the logic of this odd but the prophecy was correct. Cops nipped in and out all evening and not one of them bothered us at all despite the booze ban.

The Darkie is a fair hand at the singing and a bit of a reformed character since we had made it plain that we didn't want him with us if he was going to be an ignorant swine, which he used to be before. He had taken the trouble to learn a few songs in Italian and we soon had the locals joining in. The Darkie sang *Bandiera Rossa*, a socialist song, and about half of the cops stood up and sang along. Then we all got into *Nessun Dorma*, an incredibly difficult song to sing, but the *patron* waved us to silence as The Darkie gave a very creditable performance which earned him loud applause from the Italians.

A couple of the guys we had met were actually billeted in France, away down the coast, and they left to get a train but they soon returned with a dozen or so more thirsty supporters. A couple of them slipped out and inside about 20 minutes the place was absolutely heaving. I was still worried at this point that we were going to get nicked but as the singing swelled and more people came in it all seemed very homely and hospitable. The merriment was cut short as the *patron* hammered on the bar and shouted. The translation was that someone in the sweating crowd had stolen a gun and belt from one of the policemen. 'Oh shit,' said George, and my heart sank, but it turned out to be a case of in-vino forgetfulness, as it was on the ledge under his table. That wasn't the last we had to do with guns that night, though.

After an hour or so The Heart, Angelina and her two shadows appeared to announce that they were off to swim in the Bay of Silence. This is in Sestre Levante, of which none of us had ever heard, but they persuaded us that it was a good idea to go there. The pub was a bit overfull and a wee cooling drive in Special K's van seemed like a good idea, especially as it was so close. None of us was sober enough to drive but Ramon volunteered. Luis had one of those huge cars whose doors go '*click*' and whose every part was made one at a time by specialists and highly paid craftspeople, and we followed him. Costa and Rica were still with us and Rica said something to Ramon which annoyed him. It was something to do with Angelina and The Heart, who were snogging away in the back seat of the car in front. Ramon spoke sharply and at length to Rica and he shut up. Costa was explaining to us that Rica had said that if he was Angelina's father he'd tan her hide for her for this kind of shameless public behaviour, which was more like the Mexican and Spanish people we'd met before, but as he was leaning over the front seat to talk to George and me, Ramon told him to shut up as well, which he did. Ramon said to us, 'We protect her from harm. We do not interfere, these are the rules of her parents. It is very hard, sometimes. I do not personally approve but she is a good person. I do not know if this is true of your friend. He is a very bad liar. I saw you give him money. Get it back. I paid for the food.'

There was a sudden tension in the van and Costa and Rica were more than a bit subdued, but Anne said firmly, 'He's a nice boy. He's with us.' This was of course true, at least, the 'with us' bit, but Anne said, 'Nothing will happen to that lassie that she doesn't want to happen,' and Ramon said with a smile, once he'd understood 'This is true. She has a strong will.'

They were actually staying in Sestri Levante, in a five-star hotel called the Grand Hotel dei Castelli. It's on the peninsula from which Marconi made his first transmissions and is now, according to the informative wee booklet in the hotel lobby, 'the seat of the

Tigullio radio hams'. George said, 'Aye, its good to get your hams into a seat.' We had a wee look at the hotel while Angelina was upstairs changing and by this time The Heart had realised that, if he hadn't bitten off more than he could chew, at least there was a very large amount of masticating to be done. 'Masticating?' said John. 'Are you sure you're pronouncing that right'? Ramon was at the hotel bar and he noticed when, unprompted, The Heart came up and gave us back our money. 'I can't compete with this sort of stuff,' he whispered. 'It's just no real, is it?' Builder John commanded, 'Stop whispering. We're as good as any and better than most.' Ramon sent us over a few beers and came and joined us. 'You are staying here?' he queried The Heart. 'If I'm asked,' said The Heart bravely.

Special K, Mahoney, The Darkie and I went down the hill and, as none of us had anywhere to stay, signed ourselves into a hotel on the Baia del Silenzio called Due Mari. This means 'two seas' and when we told George where we were staying he said of Special K and me 'That will suit you two cs right enough.'

There were no other volunteers for bathing, even in romantically named bays, and leaving Luis to take The Heart and Angelina to the beach in the car we went down, accompanied by Ramon, to a restaurant and bar selected by Ramon called El Pescador. This is a Spanish name and I've no idea why, because the patron was Italian. He was named Luigi, which provoked a storm of very bad Francie and Josie impressions from the company. There were half a dozen Scots there that we didn't know, including a very distinguished looking guy in a suit that looked Saville Row and shoes that screamed 'money!' The Scotland top and the tartan tammy spoiled the sartorial effect a bit though and he was most welcoming. 'Come in lads, sit yourself down. Let me get you a drink.' He and Anne started talking about the food in the restaurant and it emerged that he was the representative in Switzerland of one of the Scottish banks, and a bit of a big Gruyere. He lives in Switzerland and had brought his wife here for a holiday. 'My goodness, when I got here was the football not on,' he laughed. His wife said, 'And I suppose it was a coincidence that you had your Scotland jersey with you?' She was very refined but pleasant and talkative and we soon, with Luigi's help, had most of the tables organised into a big semi-circle. We asked everyone else in the room whether it was okay for us to sing. 'The Gastronome of Zurich,' as George had dubbed our international banker, had made a special request as his wife had never heard supporters' songs and chants. They all said it was okay, except for a strange looking couple of guys in the corner. They didn't say anything but just looked at Andy blankly. Mahoney started with his own version of *What Do You Get*. I first heard him sing it in Spain in '82 and he adds a new verse or two every year. Here are a couple of them.

What do you get when you drink the wine?
A ten-pound fine and a year's probation
Knee in the balls in the polis station
O-o-oh, I'll never drink the wine again.

Everybody then sings 'O-o-oh, I'll never etc.

What do you get when you drink the wine?
Your shoes full of puke and a wan-night-lie-in
Seven in the morning, they fling a pie in
O-o-oh, I'll never drink the wine again.

Mrs Gastronome thought it was great. She was laughing and singing along and her husband was dead chuffed. He suggested *We'd Walk a Million Miles*, and we started off. George, Bodyswerve, Mahoney and I do a perfect (even though we say so ourselves) four-part harmony on this by adding a phrase. Everybody sings 'We'd walk a million miles for one of your goals' and we sing 'You sometimes have to' and then everybody goes 'Oh Sco-o-otland'. Ramon was laughing away like a maniac at this. 'You are all crazy. We won and you are celebrating.' He and Costa and Rica then sang what might have been the Costa Rica national anthem or a team song. We all clapped and Rica with tears in his eyes thanked us at considerable length in Spanish and finished with his only English of the evening. 'Crazy, yes. Good crazy.' He fell asleep shortly after this and missed the drama, which happened after Angelina, The Heart and Luis had come in from swimming.

As the night was draving along with sangs and clatter, as the

Bard approximately has it, one of the strange guys in the corner threw a bottle of wine at the wall. As it smashed, splashing wine and bits of glass over the people opposite us, he shouted in what I now know was Dutch. The singing stopped, but George and I tried to keep it going, hoping to embarrass him into sitting down. The strange guy then produced a gun from his pocket and peering around announced in guttural English that he was going to shoot the richest person in the room. Everybody froze except for The Heart and Angelina's guards. The Heart stepped in front of her and Ramon in front of him, with his back to the gunman, two of the bravest things I've ever seen anybody do, while Luis had his gun out, from behind Angelina. The guy with the gun didn't notice any of this byplay, however, as the Gastronome stood up in the silence as the chatter died and said, 'That will be me.' As he turned to the gunman I noticed that he too was shielding his wife. He had also picked up a bottle from the table and was holding it unthreateningly at waist level. Then John stood up and Anne, a post-feminist from way back, followed. In about five seconds everybody in the room was on their feet clutching something throwable – glasses, bottles, table lamps, knives. 'He's with us,' said Anne loudly into the tense silence. The guy slowly clocked that he wasn't going to get out unscathed. As George said later, 'He suddenly realised that if there was any scathing to be done, he was going to be the one getting scathed.'

The guy abruptly sat down and threw his gun on the table. Mahoney then started 'Spo-ot the looney! Spot, spot, spot the looney!' and everybody started laughing hysterically. While we were busy spotting the looney Ramon gathered about half a dozen of us by eye and we went over to the men in the corner. The guy with the gun reached for it but Ramon shook his head firmly and picked it up. He quickly checked it and said disgustedly, 'No bullets.' He looked as if he was going to use it to smash the guy, who had this drunken, guilty sort of look on his face, but George caught his arm and said, 'Not worth it.' Ramon nodded and hoisted the drunk Dutchman to his feet by the hair. He then took the guy's wallet from his pocket, and took all the money out, indicating to his table companion, who did the same, spilling his glass of wine in his hurry. He gave the money to Luigi, saying, 'No police' and we bundled the guys out of the door.

He then gave them a two minute warning in their own language, reinforced by a quick and very painful looking punch in the solar plexus for both of them. 'Jesus, Ramon,' said Mahoney as we went back in, 'who the hell speaks Dutch? Even the Dutch don't speak Dutch!' This is true. When you try to speak Dutch to Dutch people they always say, in about ten languages, 'What do you speak?' and then speak to you in your own language. It makes learning Dutch very difficult. It was obvious that Ramon wasn't just some bodyguard, but he said to Mahoney, 'I am a student of language,' and we went back inside.

Where everyone was a hero, especially The Heart and The Gastronome. Mrs Gastronome was dead impressed by her husband and by the tribal response to threat. She'd obviously been not completely overwhelmed by his financial success, but his physical courage had touched the places that other currencies cannot reach. She dragged him off, romance in the air and in her eyes, in about two minutes, after going round and shaking everyone by the hand, kissing cheeks, the whole bit. We saw them in Luigi's at lunchtime the next day, and sated and smug happy campers they looked. Meantime in the bar it was getting close to midnight and as Ramon went past The Heart, sitting across the table from Angelina, who was gazing at him adoringly, he cuffed him lightly and affectionately on the back of the head and said, 'Good boy – Cinderella time.' The Heart said, 'No, you go on. I'll look after her,' and Ramon and Luis left. Only as far as the car, where they sat with the doors open, chatting to John and Anne, but they left her with him, the first time she had been out of their direct line of sight since we'd met them.

In the bar The Heart had now apparently confessed to Angelina that he wasn't a rich landowner, more a kind of clerk person in a publishers. She'd obviously been filled in on this by Luis in the hotel but she acted it out brilliantly. The Heart then said he had composed a song especially for her and moved into the centre of the room to sing it. It was titled *Hello Angelina*, the Dylan song with one word changed. Before he started he said to everyone, 'Give me this one, please!' so we all pretended that we'd never heard it before and nobody joined in the choruses. He finished

'Hello Angelina, the sky is erupting, and we must be gone,' and held out his hand to her to a storm of applause, most of it for his sheer brass-necked gallusness, but a lot of it from those who'd seen or heard what he'd done earlier.

They left and another song started. The place was roaring and the air was thick with excitement and adrenalin. Hadn't we faced down a gunman? Weren't we the wee boys? Luigi appeared and pointed urgently to the ceiling saying *'pescatores!'* This means 'fishermen' in Italian and it emerged that the fishermen who had caught the fish that everyone had been eating actually lived upstairs and were up and out on the briny early doors to bring us tomorrow night's dinner. They needed their sleep. Luigi said that we didn't have to leave but that we had to be quiet, and the next couple of hours were spent in a strange and suppressed hilarity. We were all sitting whispering to each other and singing our songs very *sotto voce*, as in '*Oh Flower of Scotland*'. It was an immense strain and it was also intensely funny and satisfying. Every now and then someone would laugh out loud and we'd all point to the ceiling and hiss *'pescatores!'*

Special K sang 'Hush, hush, whisper who dares, *pescatores* are saying their prayers'. He knows every word of every verse of the Christopher Robin original and I thought Andy was going to end himself right there and then. He stuffed a napkin in his mouth and just kept getting more and more purple with suppressed laughter. Once he'd recovered he sang *The Sound of Silence*, miming every word, and we all mimed along to the chorus. Then George did an old Band of Hope song, *My Cup's Full and Running Over*, which has got all sorts of actions to be performed, and we all got into that with silent gusto.

It was getting towards 2 a.m. when Luis returned with the car, offering to take people back to Genoa, an offer that was accepted by a dozen or so. We made our way back through the silent narrow streets to the hotel, saying *'Pescatores,'* and holding our fingers to our lips. We spent three nights there, with the same kind of carry on, minus the gunman, each night. The Heart came with us to Florence but Angelina was planning to go there later and didn't want to spoil it with a four hour tour rather than a four day one, so she and her minders stayed home. Everyone spent hours practising mimes and Mahoney learned from somewhere how to juggle wet scrunched-up table napkins. The one time we broke the *pescatores* rule was when he tried it with eggs and one landed right in his wine glass, jetting purple fluid straight into George's eye. Luigi was out from the kitchen in a flash, finger pointed to the ceiling and we all whispered/roared our word. We never got to meet the *pescatores* at all but Luigi said they were properly grateful.

The next time I heard the word was in Turin, in a bar full of fans I didn't know. A big Aberdonian was shouting 'one singer, one song, please. *Pescatores! Pescatores!*' I asked him where he'd heard it and he told me it was the Italian word for '*quiet!*' and that he'd learned it in Genoa.

I don't know what happened with The Heart and Angelina but he still turns up for the games and he isn't driving a Ferrari or wearing Gucci shoes. George thinks that she is some sort of high-up politician's daughter and that Ramon is some kind of James Bond type character but nobody but The Heart knows and he doesn't talk about it. When asked he puts his finger to his lips and says '*Pescatores,* pals'.

14: A Thousand Towns

I met him in a street café opposite the Pitti Palace in Florence. A few of the foot soldiers of the Tartan Army – Bodyswerve, Builder John, Anne, Mahoney and four or five others, along with our new recruit Special K, who had driven me to Italy in a 16-seater minibus – had decided to go to Florence for the day. 'A wee bit of beauty fair makes the day fly in,' said George, who was now Lumpy George again because of the Italian mosquitos.

The game against Sweden wasn't for two days and Genoa, despite having some really smashing people and some great crack, is not the absolute architectural jewel that Florence is. We had done the walk round the Otrano, the scruffy bit of Florence on the other side of the river from all of the tourist stuff, and we had eaten a superb lunch in a really grotty cellar restaurant. The brilliant food was a surprise because the main attraction had been the fact that a sign outside announced that they had videos of all the games so far and that they did special rates for supporters. The special rate turned out to be about twice what they charged the locals but they took 25 per cent off the bill because there were a dozen of us, resplendent in our Scotland tops.

We had spent most of the afternoon in the Uffizi and in the Academy Galleries where Bodyswerve had said of Michelangelo's statue of David, 'Wi hauns that size he was probably a goalie,' and one of the female attendants had laughingly agreed. Two of the lads got on the chat with her and her pal and they agreed to show them and the rest of us round the Pitti Palace, as they were just finishing their shift for the day. My feet were knackered from the walking and from the impromptu five-soon-becoming-fifteen-a-side the night before, so when they decided to go there I walked round to it with them and some Americans we had met and sat down in the café on the broad cobbled street, while they went in.

He was sitting at another table when I sat down but he was facing me and there weren't a lot of other people around. I was sitting wishing I had somebody else's feet, with my face upturned to the June sunshine, when he came over and asked, 'Is that a soccer shirt from Scotland?' I confessed that it was and we started talking. Like most Americans he knew nothing about football, but like most Americans he was a real enthusiast, keen to learn and unusually for an American, keen to listen. His name was David Paxman and he was well into his 70s but bright as a button and funny with it. While I was sitting expounding my theories about why Costa Rica had beaten us and how, with judicious planning, we could still go on to win the World Cup, he bought me a beer without asking if I wanted one. I bought him one back ten minutes later, and we were sitting enjoying one another's company. He was telling me about his former job, about the pigeons he kept on the roof of his apartment in New York and about his youngest grandson who 'plays soccer in school with all the other pansies'.

As we spoke, a large and very noisy party of Austrians arrived. There were around 30 of them and they were awful. Austrian fans are even worse than the Germans in the arrogance stakes and their behaviour in the café was deeply unpleasant. First of all they went round hanging up all these strings of Austrian flags all over everything. They draped the trellis outside, tearing down plants to do so, and they stuck pins into the murals inside. They didn't ask anybody's permission and they leered at all the women. Most of them had rucksacks and they produced their own sandwiches and beer from them. The waiters and the *patron* weren't happy but you could see that they didn't want any trouble.

It was when more Austrians, a younger bunch, arrived and started sitting opposite the dozen or so people left in the café, staring at them and putting lumps of sugar in their drinks, obviously intent on intimidating them and in colonising the whole place, that I started to get worried. The café was half inside, half on the road and when they started moving chairs and tables to block the pavement, which ran through the middle, making people walk into the road to avoid them, I thought I would leave.

They were singing and shouting these loud repetitive songs which, even if you don't speak German, you know are filled with hate, acting like those German soldiers in *Casablanca* just before Rick tells the band to play the *Marseillaise*. David was getting very agitated. We had both given the two young blokes who sat down at our table the bent eye and I had learnt from him how to say 'fuck off' in German, a phrase that has proved useful a few times since, and they had left our table muttering.

I started to say something about leaving because the atmosphere was getting distinctly chilly, not to mention frightening, but David clamped his hand on my arm and said, 'Be a *mensch*'. I thought that he was saying 'Be a man,' but I've since learned that 'be a *mensch*' means more like 'be a real human being, you putz'.

By this time the Austrians had started throwing beer and bits of sausage and bread around. We were the only non-Aryans left in the place and the words *Skottlander* and *Amerikaner* were used often in shouted conversation which was designed to intimidate us and to insult, even though I hadn't a clue what they were saying.

Just then Special K, who is a large and sometimes intimidating crowd in his own right, emerged with several of the others from their cultural beanfeast across the road and I saw them and waved them over. When they heard the Austrians chanting they started giving it 'Scooooootland, Scooooootland' as they approached us. David by this time was frantic. 'Tell them to stop! Tell them to stop!' he said to me, pulling and pulling at my arm. 'Tell them not to do that!'

I wasn't sure if he meant us but by the time they had crossed the wide cobbled street our lot had sussed that there was a bit of soapy bubble. 'What's the problem?' asked Big Andy and I explained that the Austrians were being bastards and what had happened. As I was doing this David stood up and started shouting at the Austrians in what I assumed was German. Special K and I pulled him down into his seat but he was really angry. Anne and Builder John were trying to reason with him, making pleas for us all to go to someplace else and plans for us all to have dinner, when round the corner, in the middle of the road, came one of those stupid oompah bands, with glockenspiels, tubas etc. There were about 15 of them, nearly all hugely fat, red-faced and sweating. The Austrians went crazy, shouting and singing, and so did David.

He rocketed out of his seat and ran down the road with me and a couple of the others in close pursuit. He threw the beer from the glass in his hand all over the puzzled and angry front row of the band. 'Get out of the highway!' he kept shouting and then he started crying, a wee, old, half-drunk man standing in a foreign street facing down these bemused and beery musicians, who hadn't a clue what was going on. He was wearing a light cotton jacket and he took it off to roll up his shirt sleeve. As he thrust his arm in the face of the band leader we could see that it had a number tattooed on it. He was completely hysterical by this time. He kept shouting in what I now realised was Yiddish and the *pfennig* finally dropped for all of us. David was weeping and shouting 'We must stop them. Never! Never again'. I had him by one arm and Special K by the other 'Help me, help me' he was saying and then he said to all of us, 'Once these bastards marched through a thousand towns. A thousand towns they marched through. Stop them.' He appealed to me once again, 'Be a *mensch*'.

Special K and Big Andy had by now caught the gist of this and so had the Austrians. A lot of the Italian passers-by had stopped and a fair-sized crowd was forming. As we half-carried David back to his seat Bodyswerve and The Heart were at opposite corners of the street shouting 'Scotland. Handers. Handers!' About 20 Scots appeared out of doorways and cracks in the cobbles and ran towards us.

As we got back to the café, the Austrians were muttering. I could hear the word '*Jude*', and then two young and very drunk hooligans started going '*Jude, Jude!*' insultingly. Special K went berserk and took off for them, closely followed by Big Andy, scattering glasses and tables in their wake. They ploughed right through the crowd and got a grip of the two guys. By now there were almost 40 Scots, a dozen Americans and about double that of Italians, none of us particularly happy with this group of proto-fascists. To be fair, some of them looked a bit shamefaced and not one of them moved as Special K and Andy vanished round the corner into the alley with the Nazis. When they came back Andy told us that they had let them go after slapping them a couple of times. 'One of them peed himself,' he said with disgust, 'just stupid, stupid laddies.'

The rest of the crowd didn't agree with this verdict and when some of the very large, stone-faced Americans started picking up beer bottles by the neck and getting into some serious staring, a few of the Scots followed suit. David stood up and said to Andy, 'You didn't hurt them too much but you stopped them. Good, good. Please be peaceful now,' and he held out his arms and hugged him.

It wasn't us that started the spitting, it was the Italians, and especially the waiters. By the time the Austrians packed up their rucksacks and decamped they were totally drenched. It was in their hair, in their faces, on their food, in their beer. None of them said much, though a few of them were crying. Not a blow was struck but they were hurt more than if we had broken a few heads. The café owner turned down our offer to pay for the glasses and plates that Special K and Andy had broken. He said something in Italian, smiling a bit and one of the waiters said, 'He added it to the bill of the *fascisti*'. This prompted a few smiles and laughs and we took David to dinner and then back to his hotel. He thanked us all and insisted on paying for all our drinks as well as the food, saying, 'They won't believe this in New York, me paying.' He left for New York next afternoon, waved off by us with smiles and tears.

He told me what the word '*mensch*' meant but I learned what it really meant from his actions. David Paxman died peacefully in his chair, on his roof, among his beloved pigeons, in New York in October 1995. He was a *mensch*.

15: Estonia When You're Trying to be So Good

After the no-show no-game in Estonia, where everyone was giving Dylan's appeal to the dope-lovers of the world, *Rainy Day Women #12 & 35*, absolute pelters, FIFA in its infinite wisdom and mercy decided that these poor wee Estonians hadn't quite understood the rules, but that that was perfectly understandable, as they were after all in the same group as Sweden and it wouldn't do to just give the three points to one of Sweden's main rivals in the group.

This decision caused a lot of telephone calls to be made among our lot and there was much talk of boycotting the game, as well as of assassinating the odd Swedish FIFA official, as the SFA had bent over backwards, forwards and sideways to do the right thing and still we ended up shafted. As George said when he told me he wasn't going, quoting Dylan (nearly), 'Estonia and they'll say that it's the end, Estonia and then they'll come back again.' The upshot was that most of our footsoldiers did their voting with their feet and didn't go, for a variety of reasons, the main one being fury at FIFA and the then reasonable belief that we would hump Estonia nae tother aba, meaning more cash for the Belarus trip.

This is why I found myself at Glasgow Airport at total

sparrowfart, 6.15 in the a.m., on the day of the game in Monte Carlo, in the company of some new chums and one old one, a revered scribbler of this parish who rejoices in the Tartan Army moniker of Tumshie. He doesn't go to many games, but when he does they tend to be in sunny places while Glasgow is freezing its cojones off in midwinter. It's a knack, he tells me, and he also says that there is no corruption of any kind involved – or at least not much.

The bar was open and doughnuts and coffee with a wee splash of French brandy seemed as good a way as any of starting the day, which turned out to be long and to contain enough brandy to make any sane person snap. I certainly did. The nice man from the travel company explained that we were to be nice in Nice and we all nodded blearily and got on his nice Nice plane, but only after I had assisted the security forces with their enquiries, as some well-spoken gentleman with an Edinburgh accent had phoned and mentioned to them my past record as an international terrorist and drug smuggler. George may not have been there in body but his spirit was with us. The guys who asked me all the questions seemed to know it was a merry jape but they did it anyway and searched me and my bag pretty thoroughly, though thankfully I was spared the toley-poking. Maybe it was too early for them.

Here's a tip if you are a heavy smoker on a flight to a Scotland game abroad. Just sit in your seat and smoke as many fags as you like. If the stewardess asks you to stop just put it out and as soon as she walks away light up another one. It worked for the two guys in front of us and they must have smoked their way through at least 20 by the time we got there. I don't mind people smoking, I even used to do it myself until the kids nagged me into stopping, but the ever-thoughtful Tumshie regaled me with a myriad of stories about how planes are diverted if passengers misbehave, especially ones that smoke when they are told not to. He was well into this tale of how they just let you do it until the plane lands and then everyone on the plane is arrested and held for days, when the hugely fat guy puffing away industriously in front of us turned his head and said, 'That, by the way, is pish, pal. We dae it a' the time.' It's funny how unfriendly the word 'pal' is in the mouth of a bloke from Clydebank with an attitude, not to mention a weight problem He complained about the food as well, though how he could taste it I've no idea. It didn't stop him asking for all the uneaten stuff from our trays and from the other people round about, but it did stop him smoking for about ten minutes.

Tumshie is excellent company and he tried to keep me cheerful in the face of what I thought then was a genuine premonition. I just had this feeling of impending doom, and it intensified as we came in to land. I kept seeing the faces of people crying and sobbing and by the time we started the landing approach my brain was rattling about inside my skull like a pea in a mad ref's whistle. I felt a Corporal Fraser-like urge to shout, 'Doomed! Doomed! We're all doomed,' and I had a real job restraining myself. It was the new travel pills and the alcohol of course, as I discovered from a Scottish medical guy I met in Monte Carlo later that day, but I was totally terrified by the time we landed and it was about an hour before I stopped shaking. Once I'd had a shower at the hotel I felt better but it was not an auspicious start to one of Scotland's blacker days.

We went for a beer and Tumshie and I were just getting acquainted with the new chums when a guy called Maguire, whom I'd last met making my bed in Iceland, came over with a question, 'What's the French word for make-up, Wee Man?' I know that the word is '*maquillage*' as my French is reasonable (thank you John Cuthill, who knocked four years of it into me) and I passed it on. Two minutes later Maguire is back saying that they keep looking at him oddly in the shop and offering him lipstick and mascara and the like. He's not too happy, and he thinks he has been set up. It transpires that he wants face paints so we send him out to find a toy shop and tell him to ask for, '*peinture pour le visage*'. This worked and Tumshie gazed on aghast as about three or four tables-worth of the troops started painting each other, Braveheart-style, in preparation for the coming conflict, despatching Maguire for more as they ran out of Saltire blue. Tumshie conferred a tribal name on John Maguire after he had his full *maquillage* in place and was prancing with the others around the place, having persuaded the café owner to put John's tape of *I Have A Dream* in his machine. He is called 'Dances With Bluenoses'.

Before we got on the bus to the game some of the made-up Clydebank guys unrolled their banner, which said, 'Monte Carlo or Bust'. After the game I noticed that someone had taken the face paints to it and changed it to, 'Monte Carlo and Bust'. The trip to Monte Carlo was a joy, scenery-wise, as the road there, or the *corniche* as the French call it, is built into the coast, often over steep cliffs, and the views are totally spectacular. 'That is just absolutely fucking beautiful,' said Jabba the Hutt, as the chain-smoking Bankie was now called. He also said, 'Fucking lovely,' and, 'fucking rerr,' as other sights were revealed, but he saved his last compliment for the view straight down into Monte Carlo harbour with its mega multi-million franc yachts and sparkling azure sea, 'Whit a nice bastartin place, eh?' he said, looking around as if someone was going to argue with him. Monte Carlo is a truly pleasant place, though it helps if you have a large bag marked 'More money than I thought I'd ever need for one day'. They don't let you in to the casino without a passport, though they didn't mind the Scotland tops or the ragged kilts The seasoned world traveller Tumshie had forgotten his, so they wouldn't let us in and we were forced to sit in the pleasant square in the warm sunshine sipping beer and nibbling delicious wee nibbly things while exchanging badinage with our comrades in arms, a really bastartin nice way of spending the day. And that's not even counting the stunningly-dressed women and the swanky cars depositing people at the casino, or the millions of Japanese tourists who kept sending us over drinks and *amuse gueules* so that they could get their photos taken with us.

Growing a trifle bored with hearing *Doe, a Deer* played on the pipes for the umpteenth time, we drifted down the hill to a pleasant restaurant for a meal, much of it spent in mathematical calculations of what we needed to do to qualify after we'd got three points from Estonia. This, as George has warned before, is hubris, and sure enough, along came the Fate lady and stuck her finger up all of our arses.

That space above represents the game. It was mince. The stadium was a cheerless place with the players miles away from the troops, and the moon has more atmosphere than it has. The last time I was at a game with Tumshie was in Cyprus, and he kept bringing up the fact that we'd scored in the last second as the game dragged its weary ass to a close. One point, oh shit, more maths.

It was a doleful bus that wended it's way over the corniche in the dark back to Nice and we decided to just go straight to the bar we'd picked and get forgetful. I was well into my umpteenth brandy when a band strolled up on stage. 'That's all I need,' I was thinking, 'a bunch of Frog musos annoying me,' but their first song stopped this line of thought immediately, as the band launched straight into, 'Once upon a time, you dressed so fine, threw the bums a dime, in your prime, didn't you?' This is my favourite song of all time and its writer is my hero. By the time they reached, 'didn't you?' I was on the dance floor with two French *filles* giving it head back and plenty of shouting of lyrics.

The band were indeed French and they were called Dylan. They performed in English but it was so heavily French-accented that it made many of the songs meaningless, because the guy who was singing was just repeating the words phonetically. He saw me looking at him in exasperation and offered me the mike, in a kind of kidding way, a sort of teasing. One of the *filles* jumped up on stage, dragging me with her, and I was instantly into *Lay, Lady, Lay*. People kept sending me up brandies and I kept drinking them and singing. A wee while later Tumshie was beside me on the stage prising the mike away from my Dylan-crazed fingers and leading me homewards to think again, which I didn't until about noon, and then my thoughts were things like 'Oh no' and 'Never, never, never again will I drink brandy.' Tumshie cheered me up with what he called 'a corniche pastis', a thing with no meat or pastry but lots of aniseed and a great hangover cure.

I was on the train back from the Belarus game in Aberdeen when a guy I didn't know passed and said, 'Hi Dylan, how ye doin?' It transpired that he and his mates thought that it was my band they'd seen in Nice. 'I've never seen anybody sing Dylan word perfect for an hour and a half,' he said. 'Are you a tribute band? You were better than he is.' If Alec is reading this, that's why I rose to my feet and kissed and hugged you, comrade, because we might have only got one point in Monte Carlo, but there is a God, and he likes me.

16: The Best Planned Lays of Mice and Men

'The worst line I've ever heard was yon guy in the plane queue. Remember? He was an Aberdonian and one of his mates was saying "Would you just shut up about that quine. We're getting bored with it."' Builder John was talking on the bus taking us down to defeat at the feet of the English yet again, but we didn't know that yet, so expectation was high. 'So he turns to us and starts to tell the story of how he met this woman in Seville. You'd missed the plane, Wee Man, and we couldn't find you anywhere in the hotel, but his story ends up. "So I doggied it up a close. She was fat, like." Anne didn't talk to me for hours when I told her because I was laughing when I told her.'

'One wonders who profited from that encounter,' said George, who has remained faithful to his wife for 20 odd years of marriage and is pretty smug about it sometimes, 'and also wonders where in Seville he found a close. He was probably in the vestibule of some poor sod's house, some wee woman who was cowering behind her door wondering what all the grunting was.' He has a gift for creating a scene in a few words, has George.

He continued, 'My favourite line was when we went onto the park at Wembley to help with their grass and goal post replacement programme and that young couple were having it off on the centre spot,' he went on. 'There was this huge Saltire with a lump under it and you couldn't see what they were. We lifted it up and there they were, heaving away. Just as we did the guy looks up sideways and says "This is what I call scoring at Wembley". The girl was still laughing when we put the flag back over them. I hope they're still together. They looked a nice couple in the matching tartan. Rod Stewart was standing there as well laughing his tripes out.'

Big Andy and Bodyswerve told of the time, after that game, when they missed their transport back to Scotland, as did not a few of us, and got on a mid-morning business plane, still attired in the full gear, as the suitcases, turf, corner flags, goalposts etc. were in the bus which they'd missed after sleeping in Hyde Park. 'This guy was staring at us as though we were something his dog had thrown up. He was in the window seat with us on the two others and he called the stewardess and asked her to move him. He didn't ask us. Anyway we let him out and he sat in the aisle seat, fuming because the wumman didn't want to move him any further. She was nice, Scottish, and she thought he was being a bit ridiculous.' Bodyswerve was well into his tale. 'That's the one you asked to join the Mile High Club,' interrupted Andy, 'and she said "This is a domestic flight sir, and anyway, I'm a member already!" Oh she was a cracker that one.'

'And you said, "Fancy going haufers on a wean?" not the best line I've ever heard. It's never worked once, has it?'

'Only with Anne-Marie,' said Andy 'but she disny count.'

'That will be why you have the four weans, instead of the two she told me you were going to have, Andy, because she can't count,' said Anne.

'Anyway,' Bodyswerve went on, 'this guy was giving us the full body language rejection, though to be fair the paper he was reading said something like "Scottish thugs on hooligan rampage" which just wasn't true at all.'

'Good job he wasn't sitting with the guy with the briefcase,' said Andy.

I've heard this tale from Andy before. Apparently a sober-suited Scottish businessman waiting for the same flight as them, was challenged at the security desk after his briefcase had been X-rayed.

When opened it proved to contain nothing but a slab of turf, cut perfectly to fit in. The security man asked what it was and the guy said, "My brother is on holiday and he asked me to look after his lawn." Andy said, 'The security man just looked at him and shut the briefcase without saying a word, but I saw him pointing the guy out to his mate and the two of them laughing like anything.'

'Anyway,' said Bodyswerve yet again, 'Andy and I got a bit annoyed at this boy so we started talking loudly about what songs we should sing. He was getting interested and eventually Andy said to him, "We can't decide. What shall we sing?" So the guy says "How about something modern – *Sailing* – that's a good one and its by one of your lot, Rod Stewart".' Bodyswerve went on, 'All of this had taken ages because we didn't want to arouse his suspicions. I'm saying "*Sailing*, don't know that one" and Andy's going "Nope, nope. Doesn't ring a bell!" It had been all over the charts but this guy has decided by now that we are right eejits. Andy's saying "How does it go? Sing us a wee bit" and the guy starts going "Sailing, I am sailing" and Andy hands him a scarf so he's sitting there half crouched, moving from side to side in his seat holding up the scarf, smiling away at us "Across the sea, across the sea". Andy presses the bell for the stewardess and when she comes he says "Excuse me, could you ask this gentleman to restrain himself?" Everybody in the seats round about were absolutely pishing themselves. The mannie was furious. He ran away to the toilet and stayed there till we landed. Didn't take the joke well at all.'

Andy broke in 'Aye, we only had about ten minutes left of the flight but by the time we landed in Edinburgh we had everybody singing *Sailing* with me and yer man here in the aisle giving it pelters. What a laugh.'

'The English sense of humour is a strange thing,' said Anne. 'Do you remember the game where there was some kind of transport strike, and the taxis and tubes wouldn't go near Wembley because of us being thugs and hooligans, etcetera? John and I were staying in Kings Cross with about half the population of Scotland and we went through the station and came running out as if we'd missed the train. We climbed into a taxi and John says, "Do you ken Loch Lomond?" The man goes "Yeah, mite," with a big smile and John says "Well, could you sing it all the way to Wembley?" He laughed eventually and we had him singing it by the time we got to the pub.'

George said, 'I remember that time. We already had a bus fixed up with all our stuff on it but a Jock came running into our pub to say there was transport to Wembley for a pound. Somebody had noticed an English guy standing beside a furniture van with its back down and said that he'd give him a pound a head to take a lot of them to Wembley. The man thinks about it for a minute and agrees, but only with the van shut, in case there is bother with the police. Dozens of people come out the pub and the van's soon packed. The man collects the money, puts the back up, with lots of hands from the inside helping him, and then fastens the bolts and slopes off with the dosh because it wasn't his van. Somebody came in and told us what had happened and we went out to see. The van was rocking from side to side and all the people outside, including a lot of English people, were singing, "My old man said follow the van and don't dilly dally on the way". When they eventually got out they weren't laughing too much either but we were. Superb.'

'Going to Wembley on the tube is superb as well,' said John. 'I remember we were all packed in and it stopped at St John's Wood or somewhere like that and this frightfully posh and well-dressed lady got in. She immediately sort of drew herself up into her fur coat and glared at everybody, daring them to speak to her. Someone nearby let out a really ripe fart and just as it reached her nostrils – you could see them twitching – a guy standing next to her said "It's all right, missus, I'll take the blame for that. You don't need to pretend." She got off at the next stop, Swiss Cottage, I remember, and she wasn't laughing either, but everybody else was, including the English fans.'

'That was the 5–1 game,' said Anne, and everyone's faces went doleful, remembering the humiliation we'd felt, 'but even getting hammered didn't stop us singing. There was a bunch of people in front of us at the game singing "We'll support you up to four" and another lot on the way back down Wembley way after the game who were giving it "They couldny make it six, they couldny make it six."'

'Do you mind the drunk guy on the tube?' asked John of Anne.

'He was sitting mumbling and he's no idea where he was but he was wearing a kilt so we asked if we could help. He kept saying "It's something to do with plooks" when we asked him where he was going. We eventually went through his sporran and found a return ticket to Hackney.'

'Plooks – Hackney' said Anne. 'We thought it was hilarious but he was too far gone to care. We got a couple of guys who were going his way and they looked after him for us.'

Said George, 'I think I might have met him the next day. I was on the tube when this guy came on. He was clean and shaved but he absolutely reeked of drink and he was shivering and shaking, with his face as white as a sheet. He had a bag with his Scotland gear in it and he had a rummage through it and eventually produced a can of McEwan's Export. He looked at it and held it up and admired it for a minute or two and then he handed it to the woman next to him, a nice wee woman who was chatting away to us. He said, "Could you open it for us, hen? I don't think I could stand the noise."'

'He sounds like the Nutty Professor on the plane back from Russia,' said Andy. The Nutty Professor is a long-term footsoldier who lectures at a university and is a legend both for drinking and hangovers. Andy continued, 'This Scottish guy in Moscow had a club, and he was dishing out free booze and food to everybody. It was great and the Nutty Professor was right into it. On the way back he's sitting beside us in total hangover mode. He's white, beads of sweat on his top lip, shivering, hands are trembling, eyes rolling, not even attempting conversation, just concentrating on not being sick again. The stewardess is really pleasant and she notices his condition and thinks that he's having some sort of attack. She's read the passenger list and noticed that there is a doctor on board so she gets the captain to request his presence up front. I was playing draughts against my machine and I wasn't paying much attention but the Nutty Prof was tugging at my sleeve and Billy was asking if I knew where the doctor was as they'd been paging him for ages. The prof is retching and trying to talk and just manages to get out, "I'm the doctor," before rushing off to the bog again.'

'He's a warmer, that one,' said Anne. 'Did I tell you about the

Wembley game when John and I went to the theatre on Friday night and the man asking for the doctor? One of John's business pals had invited us to this show and it was just tripe, plain and simply awful, all about upper-class people and supposed to be funny. It was going down like shite on your shoes and in the last five minutes or so of the first act a couple of guys started butting in – "Aih say, Algernon, where have you planked my swally?" – that sort of thing. They were obviously Scottish and there for the game.

'Just as the lights went up for the interval one of them pitched forward on his face and was lying in the aisle. His mate bent over him and then stood up shouting, "Is there a doctor in the house?" and then really frantically "Is there a doctor in the house?" This chap a few rows behind us stands up and starts making his way along the row, calling "I'm a doctor." The guy that had been shouting for him then hauled his pal to his feet and said "Oh, hello doctor, this shows shite, isn't it? Do you fancy a beer?" The place just erupted. It was the funniest thing that was said in that theatre that night. We just went to the theatre bar to buy them and the doctor a beer and then went with them to the pub and had a good night.'

John said, 'Aye, David, the friend that invited us to the theatre was awful taken with them. He goes for a drink with them when they are in London. They were both medical students and one of them is a doctor in Perth now. David stays with them if he's in Scotland and at one time he had high hopes that his eldest daughter was going to marry the felly from Perth.'

'It's a great social leveller, the football,' said George. 'And it's good for romance. Do you remember Chris, the SNP guy? He's running a travel company in Estonia at the moment. He married a local lass and stayed there after meeting her in '93.'

We all have stories like this, and of the unusual retiring places and couplings between the unlikeliest people. There is for instance a Scottish bar in Tallin in Estonia run by David from Dundee. It's called 'The Pub With No Name', or at least the sign says that, it wasn't actually called anything, and it is a hotbed of international culture. On the night of the non-game, David organised a wet T-shirt competition with a prize of £200 and a trip to Edinburgh. The winner was a Finnish girl. Who lives in Edinburgh. See international culture, see wet T-shirt competitions? See coincidences?

We were picking up various troops en-route and we'd planned both lunch and dinner at stops organised by George. Man U Mike, an English guy who has been travelling with us since we met him in Slavonski Brod, had for reasons best known to himself chosen to fly to Edinburgh from Manchester to share the bus down to Birmingham with us. He had been slightly over-served booze-wise at lunch-time in the exceptionally good restaurant we'd been in, and was cupping his hand over one eye, trying to focus on the football video on the big screen. 'That reminds me,' said George 'does anybody else remember Jimmy with the patch?' Nobody did, George went on, 'I was a wee boy and it was my second Wembley trip. My uncle John told me about this and introduced me to the two people involved. Jimmy with the patch just used to be called Jimmy, but he had a glass eye. He used to put it in his pint when he was going to the toilet and leave it on his piece at work and stuff like that. One time he's at Wembley with his pal, and this trick with the eye had frightened off a woman that his pal Peter fancied.

'So they're back in their grotty room with the two beds and the bedside table in between. Jimmy takes out his eye and puts it in a glass of water before they collapse into bed. Peter wakens before him in the morning and slips the eye into a hankie and puts it in his pocket. Then he changes the water in the glass and just when Jimmy is waking up, drinks it up, coughing and choking. Jimmy is panicking "You've swallowed ma eye, ya stupit bastard" but Peter just says "We'll need to wait until it comes through me." Jimmy doesn't have another glass eye so he cobbles together a patch out of a bit of cardboard and thin strips of bedsheets, as they've no string or anything like that and off they go. Jimmy blags a big pair of yellow rubber gloves somewhere.'

'What are the gloves for?' asks Mike. 'For going through the motions,' says George, making delving movements with his hands and squelching noises with his mouth. 'My uncle John had a picture of Jimmy with his patch and the big yellow gloves round a pint. Peter lets this go on for two days, all through the game and everything and eventually comes into the pub with the eye. Jimmy takes off his patch and pops the eye in his mouth to moisten it before putting it in the socket, another one of his disgusting wee habits and Peter says "Here, I hadn't washed that yet." Jimmy was called Jimmy with the Patch for years after that though he didn't have one but according to my Uncle John, God rest him, he stopped taking his eye out.'

Man U Mike was still cupping his eye and as his sleeve slipped up his arm Anne said 'What's that, Michael?' Mike somewhat sheepishly turned his arm to let us see his brand new tattoo, which says 'Tartan Army Forever', and Sweeney, who's a charge nurse says, 'That will statistically increase our chances of ending up in a casualty ward.' He was a veritable fountain of statistics and facts on this subject. There are apparently figures proving that some unlikely percentage of the population with tattoos, far higher than coincidence could account for, end up in hospital after committing or having violent acts committed on them. 'And if they are self-administered the percentages are even higher,' he said.

George has a tattoo that he doesn't talk about much, but I got him to show it to Anne. He and his pal did one for each other when they were about 12. His pal, who according to George has been in and out of jail for years, has one that says 'Elvis'. George's is quite small and not very clear. When you eventually decipher it, you learn that it says 'Evlis'. All these years later George is still indignant. 'I didn't know that the wee bastard was dyslexic, but you would think everyone in the world would be able to spell Elvis, wouldn't you?'

John and Mike were in absolute knots, and Sweeney was saying 'and if the tattoo is misspelt you have statistically 300 per cent more chance of dying violently than anyone else.' He made this last one up, I'm pretty sure, but he told us of this guy who'd been in his ward after someone had bottled him. 'He had a whole line of tattoos of names on his arm with "Mother; Father; Pauline; Michael", about a dozen of them, but mother, father and three or four others had lines tattooed through them. I asked him about this and he said "They're deid. When they die I just get a line put through them. See that one that's all covered up? That was Angie, I kilt hur."' Sweeney looked round the circle of dropped jaws and said 'I rest my case.'

Man U Mike is a fairly unusual Englishman in that he actively wants to be Scottish, or at least not part of the English football culture. He told me once that he'd practised wearing his Scottish shirt for months before taking it to Slavonski Brod, where we first met him, but he has a Manchester accent that makes Noel Gallagher sound educated and his attempts at copying our speech patterns, which he also practices for months in private, are absolutely trouser-soakingly funny. 'Aaaahu goaaat a beeeeerd,' he announced, which translates as 'I've got a burd'. He went on, in normal Mancunian, 'And I'm bringing her a present – two presents – it's a pair of mice. She breeds them. That's why I got the tattoo done as well.'

What emerged after about half an hour's intense interrogation by Anne was that Mike, who is considerably younger than most of the rest of us, had met a Dutch girl while we were in Sweden giving Holland the fright of their lives but losing 1–0 eventually to a Bergkamp goal, and had been corresponding with her on and off since then. He's a nice lad, Mike, but very intense, and this correspondence had developed into romance, at least in his mind.

'She'll have brought her own little Dutch Cap?' joked Anne. 'Yeah, she's bringing one for me too, and a Dutch shirt,' said Mike, missing the joke entirely. 'I'm going to meet her tomorrow and give her the mice and show her my tattoo.' He was blushing furiously by now, having been sobered up by Anne's questioning, and was obviously concealing something. There was something in the way he said 'tattoo' that Anne homed in on. It transpired that Mike had told his young lady he was Scottish. 'I was wearing my Scotland top and she told me that she liked Scotsmen, so I just told her a little lie. Anyway, you told me that I could be Scottish if I wanted to. So I am, now.'

'But hasn't she been writing to you in Manchester?' asked Anne.

'Yeah, but she thinks that I just live there. She thinks that my accent is Scottish. I'll tell her when the right moment comes along.'

'We'll all back you up,' said George. 'As far as I'm concerned if you want to be Scottish, you can be. I know everyone here doesn't agree with that but at least we'll back Mike up, yes?' Even The Darkie, who has been known to utter the words 'racial purity', and who is a totally rabid nationalist, agreed, but he is a much changed man since he got married and we only have to shirrick him once or twice a trip now. 'I'm going to ask Mac to teach me to play the pipes,' confided Mike, 'so that I can serenade Beatrice. She calls herself Bee Tee.'

Mac the piper was sleeping off lunch and is probably not the man you would choose to teach you the pipes but he is almost as intense as Mike and they both relax by getting totally blootered after the game. 'Do you mind Mac took all those pictures of the pipe band?' asked Anne. This was at a Hampden game and he took two reels, 72 pictures of the band, one film before the game started and another at half time. He produced them proudly in the pub, as he is fanatical about piping and what he calls, in big capital letters, 'THE PIPER'S DUTY'. Someone asked him why he had taken so many pictures of the band. Anne was there. She said 'Mac looked at the man as though he was daft. He said "they were playing different tunes" and he was really offended when we all fell about laughing.'

Mac was also really offended, but in a different way, when the papers printed stories that he wouldn't be allowed to bring his pipes into Villa Park, as they were classified as weapons. 'There is no doubt that the pipes,' he said in one of the few full sentences that make sense that I've ever heard from him, 'are rightly regarded as a weapon of war, have been for centuries. The sound of the pipes is the song of the soul of Scotland and has led Scots to battle down the ages. It is THE PIPER'S DUTY to be with his troops, to inspire them to fight, to console in defeat and to celebrate victory. The duty of the troops is to cherish the piper. I will be taking my pipes into the ground and you will be cherishing me.'

We all agreed we would but in the event it was only paper talk, which was a good job for the Dutch, as they had bands with tubas and trombones and cymbals, all infinitely more likely to damage you when thrown than bagpipes, which was what the ban was supposed to be about. 'The day I throw my pipes at anyone,' said Mac, 'will be the day that you can put me up against a wall and shoot me. To do so would be a dereliction of THE PIPER'S DUTY, and no punishment would be sufficient.'

The rest of the trip to the hotel in Birmingham that George had chosen as our base passed in much the same way, with John telling the tale of the bunch of guys with their own piper, who had brought a wreath from Scotland to lay on the grave of Bonnie Prince Charlie when we were playing Italy in Rome. Said John, 'He's buried in the Vatican and they've got all these rules about what you can and can't wear to get in, like no shorts and no immoral clothing, really quite strict, but not an eyelash was flickered when this bunch, dressed like the day after Culloden, bare legs, ragged kilts, marched up, with the piper playing a lament. The leader of the clan is clutching the wreath, which by this time has seen a few hard knocks and looks more like a big circle of barbed wire. As they got to the gate the guards there saluted with their pikes or halberds or whatever they are, and they made a space through the other visitors. In they went at the full breenge, patriots intent on paying homage to their Prince.'

We were all feeling a wee glow of patriotic pride, smiling at John and each other, when Anne broke in, 'Yes but they hadn't been in the place two minutes before they were paying tribute to a different prince, William of Orange. Tell them John.' John said with a laugh, 'It's true. The piper couldn't resist the idea of actually being in the Vatican, the heart of the Church of Rome and he started playing *The Sash*. Very, very bad taste, but awfy funny don't you think?'

As John guffawed The Darkie asked 'Do the Swiss Guard not know *The Sash*?' One of his problems is that he thinks that Scottish minor tribal and secretarian squabbles are discussed the world over. He asked for haggis in a restaurant in Mexico. Sweeney, one of the very few of us who goes to his place of worship on a regular basis, was pretending to be outraged, but only to wind up The Darkie, at which, if he'll pardon the expression, he is a past master.

By the time we arrived at the hotel and had dinner we were all raring to go. The game wasn't until the next day and there was some serious liaising to be done with the Dutch. The local papers had had a few apprehensive headlines and some people frowned as we sang our way down the road, but most people seemed happy to see us. Then we got to the Square Peg, a bar approximately the length of Sauchiehall Street. Bodyswerve said of the Square Peg later 'It was brilliant, we fitted right in.'

Willie, one of a Perth contingent, headbangers to a man and woman, was telling of a bar they'd been in earlier. 'The full bodysearch, very thorough, but colours, pipes, tartan are okay. This one,' he said affectionately squeezing his sister Sandra, 'fancied one of the bouncers and kept sneaking down the fire escape and coming back in the front door to get searched again.'

'Very thorough,' smiled Sandra, 'and no female bouncers. I just did it at first to see if I could get out and back in. Then I wanted to see if I could cop off with him, but he never cracked a light.'

Her brother demurred. 'He knew fine well what you were up to and he played up to it like crazy, but he was one of these boys who was more interested in searching the lads, I think. They call them shirtlifters down here, not skirtlifters.'

Just then the door at the far end opened with a bang and in poured a group of Dutchmen singing '*O wat Zijn die Duisters stil?*' which is the Dutch version of 'Can you hear the Germans sing?' To which the answer in any language is 'No-o, No-o'. We immediately joined in, substituting the word 'English' for 'Germans' and contact was established without a word being said, only sung.

They really are a great bunch of people, the Dutch supporters, and unlike us, they have a team which occasionally achieves things. Apart from that, they're just like Scots except that they argue even more than we do. And do they hate Germans? Does Dolly Parton sleep on her back? If you think that the Scotland/England games are grudge matches you should hear the Dutch talk about Holland/Germany. Pieter and his pal Hans ('You'll be Hans across the sea?' asked George and Hans said 'Only when I am abroad,' setting the conversational tone) were telling us how it all got started. 'It was the war, of course. We were occupied by the Germans for five years and memories are long,' Hans said. 'They took our bikes.'

There were about a mixed dozen of us sitting round a couple of tables and all of the Dutch nodded to each other seriously. 'That's right,' said George 'the Germans confiscated all the bikes in Holland during the Occupation. Quite a sensible thing to do, in their position.' This went down like the proverbial balloonius plumbum. 'It might have been the correct thing but people were shot and killed for using a bike. We are not sensible on this subject,' said Hans. I tried to warm up the suddenly chilly atmosphere by telling them of how George was screaming for England during the 1966 final. 'Aye well,' he said then and repeated now, 'I don't remember the last time England bombed Clydebank.' This defused the situation and Hans smiled and said 'You may be getting closer to how we feel, but you are not quite there yet.'

He and Pieter were there in Hamburg when the Dutch beat Germany 2–1 to go through to the European final and according to them joy was not so much unconfined as rampant. Pieter's wife agreed. 'The boys did not come home for three days and the whole of the Nederlands went crazy. In the Leidselflein Square in Amsterdam, near our flat, people were throwing bikes in the air and shouting "Hurrah, we've got our bikes back".'

You don't really think of the Dutch as over-emotional but apparently nine million of them, about 60 odd per cent of the country, took to the streets that night in the biggest public gathering since they were liberated from the Germans. 'There was a Resistance fighter on TV,' said Margaret, saying, '"At last I feel as if we have won the war". The newspapers are normally very strict, very correct, about the Dutch team and its actions but they went crazy also. It was wonderful.'

'Your Don Howe had a heart attack at that game,' said Hans, and once we had explained that he was not 'our' Don Howe, but a self-important tube with no soul, the epitome of what we dislike about the English, Andy said 'I wish him long life to have many heart attacks. About one a week would be about right. What an arsehole he is. I turn down the sound on the Italian football when he is on.' It may be an unimportant statistic but every Scot at the table and every Scot I've talked to, when his name has come up since, does exactly the same thing, including me.

At some point in the conversation Pieter slipped out to his hotel and brought me back a book of poems about football, specifically Holland/Germany football. It's in Dutch, but it was passed round the table and people scribbled translations on it. One is titled 21-

6-88, the date of the game, and the last two lines are something like:

> *Those who fell,*
> *Rose cheering from their graves.*

There are poems by players and real poets, they told me, and one by Hans Boskamp goes:

> *Stupid generalisations about a people*
> *Or a country, I despise.*
> *A sense of proportion is very*
> *Important to me.*
> *Sweet revenge, I thought, does not matter,*
> *Or lasts only briefly.*
> *And then there was that unbelievably beautiful*
> *Tuesday night in Hamburg.*

And we think we take it seriously?

Anne was telling the Dutch about a guy she saw in a lay-by on the way back from Queretaro to Mexico City. 'There was a bus full of Germans, and this Scottish guy was parading up and down in front of it in the full Basil Fawlty "Don't mention the war" style. The Dutch, incidently, love Basil Fawlty, 'So English,' says Hans. Anne went on. 'This guy's only got a kilt, a totally filthy T-shirt, big brogues, no socks and a big feather sticking out of his headband. He's giving it goosestepping, *Sieg heiling*, finger moustache, bawling, "Don't mention the war!", every few seconds. And the thing was, he was on their bus! They'd given him a lift from the ground. And they took him back on after they'd all had their beer.' Our corner of the pub was in an uproar at this point, with Dutch and Scots striving to do a better Basil Fawlty. Pieter won, by virtue of having an excellent moustache already, and an ability to keep his face perfectly still while saying ridiculous stuff, just like John Cleese – and Jimmy Hill, of course, though he's not doing it deliberately.

Man U Mike had been in earlier but had left with Mac with Anne's practical advice ringing in his ears, 'Don't go too far away with him, he's too heavy to carry on your own. Ring us here if you can't get him home.' Mike was off to find his lady friend, as the pub he'd arranged to meet her in wasn't happy about football supporters, at least not that night. We were in it the next night and they were quite happy, though we all ended up in the Square Peg. Apart from not finding Bee Tee yet, Mike had two other problems, though he didn't know about them yet. Anne had been asking around the Dutch people and she had news 'Yes, she's here with her friend,' was the good news, and the bad news was 'and her husband.' That was problem number one and the next emerged next morning when he went to get the mice.

He appeared in the breakfast room, face tripping him and he didn't even know about Bee Tee's husband yet, as he'd dropped Mac and just gone to his bed. 'Fooking mice are gone,' he said, holding up a badly chewed cardboard box. 'I locked them in the wardrobe when we got here and the little fookers have escaped.' Anne was examining the parcel with incredulity. 'They gave you two mice in this?' Mike was hangdog. 'No, they were in separate compartments in a little cage, but the cage was too big for me bag, so I just packaged them up myself. I put in a little partition myself, as well.' Anne was envisaging chaos, 'You brought them up in a plane in this? What would you have done if they'd got out on the plane?' Mike looked defensive 'I brought them on in my hand luggage. They were fine when I put them in.' Anne wasn't satisfied, 'Mike, what do mice eat?' 'Cheese', he replied, 'and bread and stuff.' 'And what else?' asked Anne. 'I don't know,' said Mike, a bit sulkily. 'Cardboard, Mike, they eat their way through it. Have you looked all over your room?'

He had, and the wardrobe was one of those ones with no back and spaces at the sides, occasioning a glare from Anne. We turned over his bed and pulled just about everything in the room apart. Nada – the vermin had vamoosed without valediction; the meeces had moseyed, the timous beasties had buggered off, to mention but a few of the phrases mooted back at the breakfast table as we discussed how best to explain to the management that we had brought a breeding pair of mice into their clean and very well-run hotel.

'They weren't supposed to breed until Bee Tee got them back

to Holland,' sulked Mike. 'So you put a sheet of shoebox between a male and female mouse and expected them not to breed?' said Anne incredulously. 'What, did you give them a little lecture of being good chaste wee mice, or what?'

'I'll bet the little fookers are at it right now,' said Mike. 'I'll murder them if I find 'em. They were special too. Just what she wanted.' He was poised between bewilderment, anger and loss, which is why George and I went to the hoteliers and explained what had happened. They were terrific, just accepted it as part of life's rich tapestry, as the nice manager said. He also said they had cats, plural, but I didn't see any sign of them so perhaps he was just being accommodating. Which is his job, I suppose.

Meanwhile, John, Anne and Mike had been through the Thomson Local Directory and phoned pet shops all over Birmingham, to no avail. Mike said that the shop in Manchester had had to order them so they phoned there (once Mike had phoned his mum to remember the name of the place) but the woman in the shop was not optimistic. 'We had to order them from Holland,' she told Anne, much to her annoyance and to Mike's chagrin, who hadn't known this before.

'Little mice with clogs on' sang John.

'Where?' said Anne.

'Right there on the stair,' he replied and they both fell about the reception, creasing themselves. Mike hadn't heard the Ronnie Hilton masterpiece *A Windmill in Old Amsterdam*, which contains the above stanza, but Anne and John were to perform most of it after lunch to great applause, once everyone had heard the story.

Once we'd established that there was no question of replacing the mice that day, the other question that arose was how (or if) to break the news to Mike of Bee Tee's husband. We chickened out eventually, but our breastbeating was wasted. Bee Tee was well aware of the situation and had brought her pal with her specifically for Mike. Unbelievably, she was called Minne, though she wasn't interested in mice at all, but in Mike and in a few other things, none of which he deigned to share with us, though Bee Tee did once he'd gone back to Manchester. Mike and Minne are currently ongoing as of time of writing, and the plans are to meet and possibly marry in France if it can be arranged. 'Make it before the end of the first round, for Christ's sake,' said Andy, 'so that we'll all still be there.' This was after the Belarus result in Minsk.

The game that night in Birmingham was a good result for us. We couldn't have scored if we'd played all night and Holland had a stonewall penalty when John Collins armed it off the line, a fact of which we heard a lot in the Square Peg after the game. By midnight every Scot was wearing a Dutch shirt, and vice versa. We were singing 'Hup Hup Holland' and they were singing 'We're the famous Tartan Army and we're going to Wembalee.' Mike and Minne were attempting to break the world face sucking record, Mac was out like a candle in the wind while Pieter and I tried to get a note out of his pipes and George and Hans were doing a clog dance on the table, in clogs supplied by Hans. 'If we don't beat England at the weekend, I'm a Dutchman,' said George, and I said, 'me too.' Which is why we went to London twice, the first time to see what George calls the 'fat bastard manchild', score the goal of the tourney, the second to say farewell and good luck to our Dutch chums, though they begged us to stay and be Dutch with them. Both times we went South we were wearing the full Dutch kit, and so were Sweeney and Mahoney, visions in bright orange. 'If Father Byrne sees me in this,' said Sweeney, 'I'll be on my knees for a month.'

A lot more than a few tears were shed at that reunion, as the whole qualifying group and our eventual non-promotion to the next round was decided by that one Dutch goal against England. 'We would have been just as happy if it had been you who qualified,' said Pieter, and Hans, who had been spending some time with Mike, said, 'I think my friend Piet is a fookin liar, but it is almost true. If not us then you. We support two teams now.'

So do we, all of us. Even The Darkie was sad when Holland eventually lost to France on penalties, and he hates everyone in the world that isn't from Larkhall, and there are quite a few there that he isn't keen on. George calls us 'Dutchfanophiles' and it looks as if we're both going to be in Paris for the World Cup finals. If we don't qualify we're going anyway and they are coming with us. A few of us are trying to learn some Dutch, and Mac will be standing up (for once) for Mike at the wedding.

As the fans sang at Parkhead when we beat Austria:

'We're going to Gay Paree, We're going to Gay Paree
We're going to Gay Paree, but not with Michael Hirst.'

With people like that, wherever we go we can't lose. Scotland!
We'll support you evermore. Fuck the score!

Tales of
Tales of the Tartan Army

Once you've written a book like this, all sorts of things happen. TV, radio and press people phone you and ask you to share your opinion, as though it somehow has more worth than that of anyone else in the Tartan Army. They call you a 'General of the Tartan Army' and 'one of the Tartan Army's leaders'. This is total bollocks, as the Tartan Army is the only army in the world with no officers. No generals, no captains, no lieutenants. No NCOs either, no sergeant majors, no sergeants, no corporals. It is composed entirely of footsoldiers, privates marching to the beat of their own individual drums, giving and taking no orders, forming temporary and permanent allegiances as the whim takes them. It is also the only army in the world with no enemies, a fact of which all the members I know are extraordinarily proud, as we should be.

I don't speak for the Tartan Army, and neither does anyone else, so if you hear or read about somebody being called the 'commander in chief' or the 'field marshal', ignore it. In the months of the build-up to the Finals, because of the media, I met a lot of what they called leaders and they, like me, reject the title. There was a radio programme recorded in my living room with Andy MacArthur (aka The Nutty Prof.), who has written a stoater of a book about his exploits with his fellow troopers, titled *Over the Top with the Tartan Army*. Andy's been a trooper since Germany. He was asked what title he'd like for the radio show. '*Footsoldier,*' said the Prof. Wee Ian Adie, leader-aff of the Weeist (his spelling) Pipe Band in the World and the guy who patented the name Tartan Army for his scarves and T-shirts, as well as inventing the Tartan Army tartan, was there too. He's the guy on the front of this book and he's the man that the *Daily Record* decided was the 'Commander'. *The Herald* called him 'the self-titled Commander'. All bollocks. When asked, he replies, 'Footsoldier,' like the rest of us. He has had to put up with terrible crap from other Army members about this. The message is that it is not him that's doing it.

Also there was Alasdair 'More Steam' Macphail, inventor of the Tartan Navy, aka *The Friendly Isle*, his own trawler. He was asked by the programme's presenter, Billy Kay, what he would like to be called. 'Footseaman,' he replied. When pressed, he said that he would be proud of the title 'Assistant to the Chief Stoker'. Alasdair sailed his boat to France from Oban, costing himself more than a few bob in the process.

I'm proud to call these people my friends but none of us wants to be a leader, it's just that most of the media are so unimaginative that they don't grasp the point and of course once you've been in one paper, it's easier for them just to phone you rather than find their own contacts. I predict that the associations which have been formed recently, like the West of Scotland T.A., the Aberdeen T.A. and the London mob will elect officers and chairmen and the like. They will then appear on the box and elsewhere as 'leaders'. Don't believe it and 'don't follow leaders, watch your parking meters!' as the great Bob D. once said. End of rant.

Some good things came out of being the miniest of mini celebrities, though, like being asked to be on a panel in London with Jorge Valdano, who scored in a World Cup final for Argentina and who now writes on football. The bastard is also really handsome, charming, brave and writes prose that makes you sick, it's so good. The bravery comes from being an articulate and angry left-winger in a society where you can get killed for suggesting that poverty is not God's will.

He and I were on with Pete Davies, who wrote *All Played Out*, Henk Spaan, the Dutch editor of *Hard Gras*, and Adebayo Williams, the Nigerian novelist living in exile because his opinions do not coincide with those of his country's military rulers. The programme was part of a totally brilliant thing called *A Celebration of the People's Game*, a whole day of football, and our bit was called 'An Afternoon without Gary Lineker', chaired by Simon Kuper, editor of *Perfect Pitch*. It was superb. I just trashed the tabloids and predicted that England's hooligans would dominate the headlines (I claim the Cassandra prize) as well as also predicting that 20,000 Scots would travel all over France making *amis* and influencing *peuples* to be nice to each other. I can't claim the Cassandra prize for that, as she only predicted disasters. I also ventured that I thought that the final would be Brazil–France and that England would lose on penalties. There was an audience of about a thousand, mostly English punters, and I had an absolute ball.

This was a hooligan-free event in the Festival Hall on the South Bank organised by Philosophy Football, the T-shirt people, whose products include one with a quote from Albert Camus: 'All that I know most surely about morality and obligations I owe to football,' and one from George Best, which is: 'I spent a lot of money on booze, birds and fast cars. The rest I squandered.' There were thousands of people there, with live poetry, five-a-side, table football, quizzes, plays, videos of every game you've ever wanted to see and real celebs, like George Best and Jim Baxter, as well as paintings and films. It was football saturation and it was a day to remember. They're going to be doing it again before Euro 2000 and I cannot recommend it highly enough. They even hired a piper, Willie Cochrane, and he was superb as well.

The night before, Philosophy Football put me up in a hotel and I had a pint with Johnny Haynes, John Charles and Jim Baxter, three gods from my boyhood, and they turned out to be just as interesting as I'd hoped they would. These guys have seen it, done it and not only got the T-shirt, but have been on the go since before T-shirts were invented. (Remember vests? and liberty bodices? There was a misnomer, because there was nothing more restricting than a liberty bodice.) All three agreed that Hoddle had been right to drop Gascoigne. 'If he's no' fit and won't train right, then he deserves it,' said Baxter. I just stared at him, the greatest non-trainer and pint-sinker in football history, and he had the good grace to smile, but he repeated his comment in front of about a thousand people the next day without the glimmer of a smile. Everybody was nodding seriously and I was thinking that Slim Jim still has the chutzpah, enough of it to sell a dummy still.

There was another spin-off from the book, when a guy called Iain Gordon, Manager of the Pavilion in Glasgow, uttered the most expensive sentence I have ever heard. It was, 'Why don't you turn the book into a play?' I did, and there now follows a blueprint of how to lose £37,000, which you don't have, in eight weeks.

First you need a director. I'd met and interviewed Martin McCardie professionally when he was directing shows for his own company, Wiseguise. I've always been impressed by his work, and he's now writing film scripts and TV serials and plays, and acting and directing, and he's going to be mega-famous one of these days. I phoned him and sent him a copy of the book, and he phoned me back a day or so later to say that it was the best football book he had ever read. This is no small praise, as Martin has read just about every football book ever written and doesn't flatter people. If anything, he does the reverse. When I finally finished the script we had a meeting in a pub (we had all our meetings in pubs) and he said briskly, 'Look, the second act is a pile of shite. You'll need to write another one.' So I did, and then he added bits of his own and rewrote it, adding bits that the actors put in and chopping ruthlessly when he felt it necessary. The final result was a collaboration that owed as much to him as it did to me and it was excellent. Every single person that I've talked to who saw it loved it.

Despite the advice of my theatre-directing buddy, Special K, who has appeared in previous stories, I went ahead and promoted the play myself. Iain Gordon had misgivings about this, too, which he was delighted to share, and they were both right and I was wrong, but what the hell, it really was a good play. I thought that I was going to make a hundred grand and the plan was to take the cast and crew with me to France, where we would play in theatres in St Denis and St Etienne. BBC Scotland were also going to make a TV documentary about it and even offered, after some negotiation, to pay us £5,000 for doing so. As I said, I ended up losing a lot, which has meant remortgaging the house and trying to sell the family dacha in Millport, which at the time of writing is still for sale and is a v. des. res., if you want a wee, cosy, old-fashioned house with a suntrap of a back garden. Still, if you are going to play big boys' games, you have to play by big boys' rules, and I am proud to say that everyone got paid, every last penny – except the Royal Bank of Scotland, which is still waiting, more or less patiently, for me to sell the house in Millport.

Putting on the play was the best fun I have had in ages and I'd like to thank everyone concerned, with one exception, who knows who he is, and who, as his life sours around him and his hopes and dreams dry up and blow away like spores from a particularly fetid mushroom, will someday find out that I am behind the colour going out of his existence and will then kill himself in a particularly unpleasant way. Just kidding. Not.

The rehearsal period was fascinating, watching the actors struggling to make the lines sayable; and the jockeying for positions and for better lines by the nine members of the cast had only one of them storming out. That was Billy Riddoch, mentioned in an earlier story as Billy the Actor, but he and I went to a Motherwell game and Martin got things straightened out. It was my own stroke of genius, that, the Motherwell game, because their games last season induced a trance-like acceptance of just about anything and those who saw them will say and do whatever is necessary so that they don't have to go to another one. Unless of course, like me, they are supporters and linked by psychic ties which are stronger than the steel which the town of my birth no longer makes. Billy was fine after we'd wakened him. He just said, 'Yes, yes! I'll do it! No more Motherwell, please.'

Billy is one of the world's great guys. He cares deeply about his art but he can also take a joke. He let me write his programme notes for the play and then didn't kill me. They went like this: 'Billy Riddoch has worked in most theatres in Scotland: once. With that crisp and accurate timing for which he is renowned, he left Aberdeen just as the oil boom started and has lived in the Lowlands ever since. He is probably best known televisually not as a Teletubby, though the resemblance to La-La is remarkable, but as the senior of the two Lachies in *Hamish Macbeth*. He is currently holding himself in readiness for Holyrood. He has been cautioned several times for this by the Biggar constabulary.'

He played Builder John in the play and he was terrific, as was everybody else. Outstanding memories of the two weeks at the Pavilion, one at the Royal Lyceum and one at Cumbernauld, are artistic, personal and financial. The first night at the Pavilion was a joy, with the place packed to the rafters, my whole family there, me and Martin sitting nudging each other as the audience laughed at our lines, the overwhelming applause at the end and the sheer soul-satisfying feeling of having done it. I also remember seeing Billy McNeil crying during the scene about Jock Stein's death and Laurie Ventry, who played George, thanking me with tears in his eyes for writing the lines that he had to say in that scene. Supporting Celtic is a way of life for several of the cast members, not to mention the director, but a couple of them told me that being part of it had turned them into better Scotland supporters as well. You can't buy that sort of stuff, or the respect from folk like Special K, who not only told me that it was a really good play, but who, on hearing of my financial situation, lent me three grand from his own pocket to pay that week's wages for the cast. Craig Brown wrote to me as well saying that his family, one of whom got peripherally involved, had really enjoyed it.

His daughter got involved in a roundabout way. One of the weird spin-offs from writing the book was that six different people sent me World Cup songs, presumably because they thought that I had some influence with the company in England who were making the decision. I forwarded all the songs that I received to the company, or advised the authors to do so, but I took a real liking to one of them and decided to use it in the show. It was titled 'Skinny Malinky Parlez Vous', by a Borderer called Doug Mann, and I thought, and still think, that it is a great song. He and I had more than a few mutually supportive conversations and he eventually got to record it via Ronnie Simpson at Lismor Records. He also almost got to appear on *The Big Breakfast* singing it. I'm afraid that I decided against appearing on *The Big Breakfast*, though I was asked several times, on the grounds that I saw it once and found it abysmal.

It was ages ago and it might have improved but I'll stay happy in my ignorance, thanks.

One day when I was talking to Doug he told me of a call he'd had from a pleasant lady called Val Sutherland. She's a teacher at Coylton Primary near Ayr, and she had phoned to ask if her pupils could sing his song at their school concert. Doug instantly agreed and then a thought struck him. There were three copies of the song. I had one, he'd sent one to the SFA and he had the other one. Where had she heard it? She said, 'My dad plays it in the car. He thinks it's great and so do I.' Her dad is of course Craig, who had blagged the tape when it arrived and had been heard humming the song by Val.

We had great fun playing the songs I'd been sent, while bombing down various French motorways; and we also got a CD called *The Tartan Army: Scottish World Cup Anthems* which is a pleasure to listen to: some of: once. But we played it so many times that I now, I'm ashamed to confess, know all the words to 'Big Trip to Mexico' and 'Say It with Pride', two songs of truly appalling terribleness. Bizarrely, I'm actually singing on the second one, as my next-door neighbour, Brian, owns Ca Va Studios, where it was recorded by the Scotland squad in 1990, and he phoned me and asked me if I wanted to come along and join in.

But I'm getting ahead of myself again. Another wee adventure that I had because of the book started with a phone call from a really nice guy called Iain Falconer, who is an oil trader (with a very convoluted CV) working out of London, and who is now another member of the Tartan Army, Losing a Gob of Dough by Putting on a Show Division. He and his mate hired the Buddha Bar in Paris, a very ritzy wee *boîte* indeed, for the night before the Brazil game and it was madness writ large, with just about everybody but me and the two organisers more blitzed than Clydebank, Coventry and London combined. Sean Connery was up on stage, though there hadn't been any plans for him to be, totally steaming, trying to calm down the hordes who had been attacking the free bar for hours. He was going, 'I'll teach you all a Scottish word, an old one. Is everybody ready? – WHEESHT! I'll say it again – WHEESHT!' You have to imagine in your mind's ear exactly what the word 'wheesht' shounds like when shaid by Sean. And that wasn't even the strangest thing that happened that night. Iain had promised me £100 if I would come and read one of the 'Tales of the Tartan Army' to the audience in the Buddha Bar and I, being more than a bit skint, as well as a bit of a show-off, agreed to do it without thinking about what it would be like, not to mention the fact that I had never done anything like it before. I still haven't, as a matter of fact, though obscure libraries in the Borders and East Lothian keep trying to get me to come and do it. I will, if I'm asked nicely and somebody pays my fare, but it hasn't happened yet.

Anyway, I'm there hours early, dead sober, and absolutely paralysed with stage fright. I keep seeing people I know and haven't seen for ages but I can't concentrate on talking or listening to them because the adrenaline has me gabbling like an eejit. I do remember meeting Ian Reid, the guy who faced down the gunman in Sestre Levante, and his smashing wife, because they phoned me after Ian had recognised himself in the book, and they came to the first night of the play in Edinburgh. They also brought me their Sweden jersey from 1990 to add to my collection, a truly generous gesture, and if I didn't thank them adequately at the time, I wish to say now that I am deeply grateful for the thought and for the jersey, which is on the wall of my room.

I was introduced to Rory Bremner, who was the MC for the evening, and who looked at me a bit keenly, I thought, when he heard that I was going to read a story lasting nine minutes, but he nodded and said that he'd introduce me and try to keep them quiet. The noise level kept going up as Kenny Dalglish arrived, and then Ally McCoist and Fred MacAulay, whose show I'd been at the night before, halfway up the Eiffel Tower, while the footsoldiers outside sang, 'Only a pylon. It's only a pylon. Just a big fucking pylon, oh, it's only a pylon', to the tune of Guantanamera. Others were singing 'Guantanamera, there's only wan tanamera.' Both of them were steaming by the time they got to the Buddha Bar, as was Ewan MacGregor, who took off his kilt in the lift for reasons best known to himself. The lad is, as they say, not under-equipped, but then I knew that already, as he'd flashed the entire studio audience on the *McCoist and MacAulay* show the night before as we sang, 'We Love Jimmy Hill, he's a god, he's a god.' I didn't see the broadcast version of the show but I'll bet that Ewan's family jewels didn't feature. His own family did feature, though, as he got his mum and dad out of the audience, and right jewels they turned out to be. They were brilliant. After Ewan had lifted his kilt there was much banter about the size of the wedding tackle on view and Ewan's dad said, 'Oh, yes, he gets it from his dad.' At this point Fred said, 'Is that right? Yes, they told me that the families up there were close, but they didn't say they were that close.'

Meanwhile, back in the Buddha Bar, I had found a storeroom in which I wished to hide to take me away from the temptations at the bar and to conceal the chattering of my teeth. In said storeroom were members of Macumba, a Scottish samba band who had been brought to France by an organisation called Scotland the Brand, and whom I was to meet again all over the place from fancy châteaux to tents. They are really nice people and they chatted away to me to try and take my mind off having to go out and read my story to the now roaring mob. Stage fright is horrible and I wouldn't wish it on anyone, except for the guy I mentioned earlier, who knows who he is, and that would be quite a good way for him to die, nauseous and gasping for air. I went out into the bar again and by this time they'd let the bears in. They'd already heckled Rory Bremner off and were throwing beer and shouting at Big Tam Connery. At that moment I totally bottled it. I was tempted just to run out but I responsibly looked for the chap who was what passed for a stage manager in the chaos and found him looking for me with both of us going, 'No, I don't think so.'

At that point it was around midnight and I dived head first in to a big bottle of something or other while going round and talking to the people I hadn't been able to earlier. Macumba came on and quieted the hordes for a bit and then Ian Adie with the Weeist Pipe Band in the World. He was an absolute hoot. I put the two Ia(i)ns, Falconer and Adie, together and I'm glad I did because they and the pipers were just what the Buddha Bar needed at that moment. It's a difficult scene to describe, but if you can, imagine a room about 60 ft x 80 ft with a big broad balcony running all the way round, with a free bar the full length of one side with a few tables and chairs, all absolutely stuffed full to bursting with shouting, happy, sweating members of the Tartan Army. The whole room was dominated by a giant bronze buddha about 20 ft high with

Ian Adie, blue face aglow with excitement and effort, hanging off it and conducting his band as the room roared around him. It was the scene for which the word 'colourful' was coined. 'Rabelaisian' is another word that suits. Can you imagine standing in all this chaos and a somewhat pished Ulrika Jonsson coming up to you and saying, 'Why don't you grope me too? Everybody else in the place has,' and you don't? I know a man who did, and he still talks about it. I can't remember leaving the place, but outside the streets were still full of Parisians left over from the big parade and I sobered up while doing the conga with a bunch of them before wending my way, via several café-based divisions of the lads, to my hotel and peace and sanity.

There are two happy footnotes to the Buddha Bar, as when I got to Bordeaux I found that Iain Falconer had spent a considerable time trying to find me in order to give me the £100 which he'd promised me and which I hadn't even performed for. The whole gig lost him and his mate about £10,000 but he does not regret a penny of it and neither he should, because it was a one-off, a truly unique event. I went round to the office he'd hired in Bordeaux where he was sitting on the phone talking in several of his half dozen or so languages. Hand in pocket. Thousand franc note. Thumbs up. One of nature's gentlemen. Another of nature's gentlemen also found me in Bordeaux. Ian Adie came up to me as I was standing slightly puggled in one of the tents that were such a joyful place to meet people and said, 'We made enough to pay for the trip out of the Buddha Bar gig. Here's your bit. Get a round in and no crap about giving me back change.' And he gave me a thousand francs as well. This kind of generosity can only be accepted in the spirit in which it is offered. They both knew I had hardly any dough and they made me take some of theirs with grace and style. That is class, and so were all the other people who came up to me and invented tenners and twenties that they owed me, as well as buying beers and paying for meals before I had a chance to. I was brought up to believe that debts are always paid, but the debts I owe these guys are more than cash. There's a shining bright thread of generosity of spirit that runs through the Scottish character and particularly the troops of the Tartan Army. These people are exemplars of it and I am uplifted by them. It goes something like this: 'The guy is down. Get him up and hold him till he is okay.' No hesitations or questions in between. Needs help. Help. As my old man used to say, 'Ye cannae whack it.'

Another example of generosity when I was supposed to be reading from the book was in Bordeaux, when Scotland the Brand, in the person of the lovely Alice, invited me to a château owned by, and I'm not kidding, Jean-Marie Johnston, an umpteenth generation French–Scot whose ancestors went to the area after the '45 and ended up owning big dauds of the countryside, the way that most Scots seem to when they are exiled. Jean-Marie was generosity itself and heaped coals of fire on the heads of a bunch of people from a well-known company who should have known better but who were apprehended drunkenly passing bottles of Jean-Marie's excellent claret out of the back window of the château and into their van. He went and got them a whole case, which he presented to them with a flourish and a very Gallic and Gaelic smile. Tumshie said, 'I really have to write something about his. How can I resist the temptation to say that they were caught claret-handed?'

Alice insisted that I come anyway, even though the reading was cancelled, and when I found out that there was also to be a whisky tasting, not to mention free Scottish lamb for tea, plus bagpipes, I was extremely keen, as I am one of the keenest whisky tasters I know. Tastity taste, I went for a while, and then it was sitteddy down somewhat abruptly to prevent the fallingty down. Then it was dancity dance and singity sing. I even sang along to a banjo, played by one of the kid-on Tartan Navy, a bunch of Aberdeen fishmongers heavily subsidised by the aforementioned company and about as much fun as a wet weekend watching paint dry. I am pissed off at them because they hijacked Alasdair's concept and then didn't even sail all the way and I am even more pissed off at the brewery because I know Alasdair was in touch with them in search of a few bob for diesel. They claim that they got both applications on the same day. The thing that I am most pissed off about, however, is that bloody banjo. When I get to Hell the wee imp will open the door and say, 'Welcome to Hell. Here's your banjo.' I hate the instrument with a passion and after that night I seemed to be attached to that banjo by some kind of psychic umbilical cord. Everywhere I went these guys were there, plucking away. They even produced it on the bus to the Norway game and, despite my trying to throw myself off the bus while it was going, insisted on playing it. Pete the Prod made up a great song for that bus but those eejits and their stringed monster drowned it. Here it is, to the tune of 'You Canny Shove Your Granny Aff a Bus'.

> I'm no a Brazilian, I'm a Scot,
> I'm no a Brazilian, I'm a Scot,
> I'm no a Brazilian, I'm wan in five million,
> I'm no a Brazilian, I'm a Scot.

The Norway rhyme is, 'I'm no Norwegian, in fact I am Glaswegian,' and the Moroccan one is, 'I'm no Moroccan, you must be fucking joking.'

Genius smothered by mediocrity, it was ever thus, and I'm quite glad that I sang 'The Northern Lights of Old Aberdeen Mean Sweet Fuck-all Tae Me,' and I'm also glad that they noticed.

It isn't all sweetness and light, but it is a laugh.

Let Me Through, I'm a Doctor

People change, and it would be fair to say that I returned from our campaign in France as a completely different person. This was because at 3.30 in the morning after the Morocco game, in an underground car park in the middle of St Etienne, I swapped my passport with a kind and distinguished gentleman called the Frying Doctor. He gained this sobriquet because of his cooking capabilities and the fact that his profession takes him all over the world, as he has very high-level medical skills. He is also a genial and genuine headbanger, a true footsoldier.

It seemed like such a simple idea at the time. The Doc had a ticket but didn't want to go to Scotland right away and I had no ticket, about twenty quid, a walletful of trashed credit cards and an uncontrollable desire to get home, curl up in a corner and weep for several days. As the brandies went down and the lamentations increased, the swap seemed not only logical but completely and utterly necessary. It became my manifest destiny. The fact that he is tall, dark-haired, glasses-free and distinguished-looking suddenly had no relevance. I am none of these and have no medical experience of any kind except for knowing when to take Alka

Seltzers (as soon as you wake up or before, if possible), so I was definitely getting the best of the deal. Or so I thought.

The F.D.'s ticket and passport safely pouched, I made my way home singing to my digs. The singing woke my hosts, a well-to-do and pleasant couple called Blanc who had been assured by the St Etienne Tourist Office that there would be no hooligan behaviour and who had consequently opened their very luxurious house, complete with swimming pool, as a very up-market, one-person B&B. The tale of how I lucked into this is convoluted and involves chicanery, though only a little on my part. I had planned to waken them anyway, as I needed to leave at 8 a.m. to get a train to get a bus to get a train to get another bus to the airport. They were full of commiserations and I was full of brandy, so they let me sing the 'Marseillaise' once more and put me to bed.

Madame Blanc made me eat my *petit déjeuner* the next morning before her ever-helpful husband took me down in his car and bundled me onto the train, having offered to buy my ticket if I was stuck. On the train I pondered, as much as one can when wedged in with a mixture of singing and shouting Tartan Army and wee toty French school kids with fascinated and scared big eyes. Sweeties and chocolate were hurriedly purchased at the first stop, while we held the train doors open to prevent it leaving, and were duly distributed to the kids with the help of their teachers. What I was pondering about was what actual crimes I was committing and what penalties I might incur if I got caught. I decided that to protect the Doc I would say that I had found the passport and the ticket in a café. This, I later discovered, meant that I would be confessing to theft, fraud, illegal immigration, impersonating a doctor and sundry other misdemeanours, most of them near-capital crimes in France, where they take the question of identity and of who you are very seriously indeed. Just look at Sartre.

When I got to the airport I met young Spider, a new chum whose real name is Jamie, but who had been reporting back from the Tartan Navy via the Web and who turned out to be a lad to walk a mile with, as sailing from Glasgow across the Channel and then up the Seine in the dark with the mad pirates on board Alasdair Macphail's boat would have tested the fortitude and patience of an entire pantheon of saints. He was just about running on empty and stared at me wearily when I told him of my cunning plan, slowly shaking his head in disbelief, but his advice was sound: 'Don't, for God's sake, tell anyone else,' he said. Good advice, but unheeded, as I told every Scot I met, none of whom said a dicky. Now I know how Bonnie Prince Charlie must have felt during his escape.

The first hurdle was the ticketing desk. I produced ticket and passport with a flourish and was immediately told that I could leave on an earlier plane if I wanted. I said *oui*, and was ushered through to the reception lounge. When the plane was called I bounded up to board. A mistake. Enthusiasm in airports is apparently the opposite of de rigueur in France. Everybody looked at me and as I walked through at the head of the queue the seriously-armed soldier two metres behind the desk barked, 'Votre passeport?'

There's the cop's hand on the shoulder when you've got dope in your pocket, falling out of bed, the guy turning over four aces when you've got four kings, the girlfriend saying, 'I just don't love you anymore,' and then there's that 'Votre passeport?' I would settle for any of the first four or any combination of them, rather than go through those few seconds again. I turned my head in profile, pretending to search for the way to the plane, and resolutely avoided his eye, holding out my empty hand for what seemed like forever as he studied the Doc's picture. He handed it back with a smile, saying, 'Vive l'Armée Tartan,' and I still don't know if he knew or not. It was probably getting near the end of his shift.

The next hurdle was the ticketing desk at Charles de Gaulle in Paris, having overcome the minor hurdle of having to find it, as we landed at a totally different airport. I'd chummed up with a large guy named Bouncer who had walked down the aisle on the Lyon–Paris plane asking, 'Anybody here speak French', which I'd thought was a kind of daft question, as everyone on the plane did. He needed a translator to chat up a very attractive and chic *femme* who had had the misfortune to be seated beside him. He's from somewhere near Aberdeen and his problem (and the lady's) was that his English is not English as it is spoken worldwide, but a broadly-accented Doric which even this fellow Scot had difficulty with bits of. I got 'Furryboots ye fae?' across successfully, to which the answer was Paris. She then had a question of her own, which was, 'What language does your friend speak?' I explained it was a variant of Scottish English – a kind of patois. 'Not gayleek?' said the lady. 'It is not gayleek?' Once I had understood that she meant Gaelic I reassured her. It then emerged that she spoke more than passable English, albeit with a heavy accent, and as the same applied to Bouncer I explained the situation to both of them and left them chatting away slowly and clearly to each other. The last thing I heard and saw was Bouncer asking, 'Nae merrit, like?' while clasping her hand and pointing to her ring finger, to which she replied, 'I cannot marry you. I 'ave an 'usban'. That seemed like a suitable point at which to leave them together, and I am absolutely certain that they both knew fine well what the other was on about, because as we were deplaning in Paris, I heard her say, 'you 'ave two 'ours only, I know an 'otel.' The huge wink I got from Bouncer was a bit of a giveaway as well, not to mention the fact that they left in her car.

Bouncer's mate Kenny and I went for a beer once we'd got to Charles de Gaulle and his advice was, 'Brass it, but don't tell anybody else.' Too late, as by this time I was Doctor Wee Man to half the Scots in the airport, nearly all of whom, naturally enough, were in the bar. They agreed to let me go up to the check-in on my own and the plan was that if it looked like there was going to be hassle, they'd create some sort of diversion and I could maybe fade away. One of this motley crew, hardly any of whom knew each other, was at the bar creating a small diversion of his own. He was saying, 'Is this Mars Bar for sale?' pointing to a box half full of them. He repeated the question in French and on being told, '*Oui, Monsieur*,' with a kind of puzzled look, he strolled off, saying over his shoulder, 'That's good. I'm just going to check out a few more Mars Bars first. I've a few other Mars Bars to look at.' He repeated this in French as well, to the great hilarity of the bar staff, who then tried to sell all of us Mars Bars, pointing out the high-quality toffee, the great chocolate, etc., and doing over-the-top selling like crazy, all very un-French and very funny. They took the box over to the guy and he solemnly went through a dozen or two, holding them up and comparing them, before choosing what he declared was, 'a bargain in a chocolate and toffee confection, and you'll notice that we are all now receiving completely excellent service'. This was true and we'd also collected a bit of an international audience, which was not my plan at all, as everybody was singing, 'Mars Bars, Mars Bars,' to the tune of 'Irn Bru', the song of the 1998 World Cup.

I sloped round the corner to the ticket desk and presented passport and ticket to a pleasant lady in her forties who welcomed me effusively. 'Bonjour, Docteur. How are you today? Nice to see you,' and other stuff, all very unlike the usual professional smile and ritualised courtesy. I was, of course, completely paranoid, thinking it was designed to distract me while the gendarmes were summoned, but what she wanted to do was to introduce me to Madelaine, their new trainee, who was going to go painstakingly through every jot, tittle and jaunt of the Doc's itinerary over the past months, so that she could practise the various international ticketing codes, taking twenty minutes for something which normally takes about thirty seconds. I didn't know this at the time, but ten minutes into, 'And after you left Peru, Dr – , when did you get to India?', with me not knowing the answers, my arse was busy making shirt buttons. I kept saying, 'I don't remember, check the list.' By this time I was wringing with sweat, huge patches under the arms of the Scotland jersey, running down my face and dripping off my chin, and my eyes were flickering all round the room, waiting for doom to arrive, while my knees trembled and my hands shook. It suddenly occurred to me that the people who were watching the TV monitors which they have in every airport were examining a guy who was looking and acting like the guiltiest person in the world and, even though I say it myself, in an inspired piece of improvised, though probably unnecessary arse-saving, I sagged against the counter and blew fresh beer and stale brandy fumes all over Madelaine, while apologising for having 'une gueule de bois', literally 'a mouth of wood' and French for a bad hangover. Both Madelaine and the other woman were instantly solicitous, the elder explaining to Madelaine that Scotland had lost the night before and that most customers with hangovers were not nearly as pleasant as the *Docteur*, who was obviously suffering. I was ushered over to a seat, a glass of water and an excellent coffee provided, and Madelaine sat across from me finishing her paperwork.

Then the other woman came back smiling triumphantly. 'Club Class, Docteur. We have obtained for you Club Class! No extra charge.' She must have pulled some string or other. Then her face went doleful and she explained, 'But we are having a problem with getting you to Edinburgh. All the seats are full up with people. Perhaps you could go to Glasgow and travel to your home from there? It would help us so much, Docteur.' This news caused me the worst poker-face problem yet. I'm quite good at hiding apprehension, fear and sadness – I am after all a member of the Tartan Army – but there is nothing in my background or training to help me hide joy and happiness. I did, however, manage it quite well, I think, as I said in a judiciously helpful tone, 'Oh well, that will be all right, I'll manage,' while my brain was turning wee joyful cartwheels and shouting, 'Ya beauteyyy.' There are times when I really do think that God is a Scot, though they are few and far between when following the team. This was one of those times.

Because I had been away from the cafe for so long, ones and twos of guys kept drifting past the desk and where we were sitting, going, 'Hello, Doctor,' and, 'Everything all right, Doc?', 'til eventually there were seven or eight of them standing nodding encouragement and giving me the thumbs up. That loud whining noise that you just heard was the paranoia kicking back in, smashing its way up through the gears until we were in fifth with the engine revving and screaming. I was waggling my eyebrows, my hands twitching desperately while I tried to stop them making shooing-away motions, when Kenny eventually got the message and dragged everyone off. The older lady said to Madelaine in French, 'You see the respect, the liking of the friends of the Docteur?' She said to me, 'Your friends are caring for you, *non*?' I nodded and tried to look like someone everyone respected and cared for. This is fairly difficult to do while wearing a Scotland jersey which has hardly been off your back for three weeks and which has the red-haired wee cardboard Jimmy badge, the one the SFA issued all of us with, which has been attached to said shirt for the same length of time and is not looking in the best of health. It says on his shirt, '*Oui, mes amis*. I won't let the side down,' and as

Madelaine leaned over and read it out loud, I experienced a minor frisson of doubt. Was this jaunt a kind of hooliganism? If I got caught, would I be letting the side down? Later in the café my new comrades in arms pooh-poohed this negativity. The Mars Bar guy, Buckets, asked, 'Who are you hurting? Not us. We think you are totally fucking crazy and we kind of like that. Not the airline. The seat's already paid for. It's the bureaucrats, the people with a vested interest in keeping nationalities apart, like these stupid segregation efforts at the games, they're the ones that will be wanting to give you a doing. You're not letting the side, or us, down. Us, we'll support you evermore.' And they sang it while I sat with tears in my eyes.

Before that I had one more barrier to cross, in the shape of a young English ticket person at the airline desk, the one who actually allocates you a seat on the plane and labels your luggage. I'd just finished getting my new Glasgow itinerary from Madelaine, been waved off with multiple '*au revoirs*' and '*bon voyages*' and gone round to the desk. The young, blond, sharp-looking guy didn't look like your average ticket clerk. He looked like all the guys that Nigel Havers ever played in the movies, the charming Aryan amateur. He looked, in fact, quite a lot like Prince William, the one who will be King Billy V (and won't the North of Ireland be pleased). As soon as he opened my (or the Doc's) passport I said, 'Well, your Highness, slumming it for the day among the French peasantry, are we?' The thing was, he knew right away what I was talking about, 'Yes', he said, 'people do say I look like him.' This may well have been because the hair was exactly the same colour and cut as our glorious leader-to-be and I had a strong feeling that this was not a coincidence. I was telling him that he should be selling himself as a look-a-like for opening fêtes and stuff like that and he was saying, 'Yes, I've seen a lot of him in magazines – my sister's.' This last came a little too hastily and he coloured a bit as he handed me the passport back. The lad may have wanted to look like the Royal Parasite, or Not Free Willy, but I had the strong feeling that it wasn't girls that he was trying to attract. Prince Wills as a gay icon – there's a thought.

As we trailed through to the departure lounge when the departure time was announced, I discovered that there were only five or six of the café bunch on the Paris–London flight, and they were all people who had been on the phone to book right after the game. Buckets was one of them and he kept saying, 'Go on – you've got a Club Class ticket – get in their lounge and tell us what it's like.' I went in, having to subject my ticket to scrutiny and to some fairly serious disapproval by the small Oriental guardian of the sacred portals – as he obviously regarded them. Once in, and feeling hassled, as I had noticed him letting other people through with not even a cursory glance, I got myself a free beer and sat down to take stock.

Two minutes later I was out of there, feeling a bit like a Mississippi Negro at a Ku Klux Klan rally, or the guy who passed the port the wrong way at the university top table. The sheer blast of animosity was astounding. All these men in suits and the few very elegant women just stared at me as though a bad smell had entered the room. In retrospect, given the length of time I'd been wearing my top, maybe it had, but that doesn't justify the total bristling hatred. One large English guy stared at me in disbelief, got to his feet and said to his companion in that loud bray that can fill an aircraft hangar with postulated and posturing superiority, 'Some mistake here,' as he moved to the doorkeeper to query my right to entry. Ordinarily, of course, that would have been my cue to scratch my arse, fart, sing, 'If you hate the fucking English, clap your hands,' be offensively gregarious and ogle all the women, as I am a great man for the reinforcing of social stereotypes when I encounter this class shite, but I wasn't in a position to have my credentials checked and nary a one of these gimlet-eyed trough-guzzlers was going to believe for an eyeblink that I was an international medical consultant. The English class system seems to have gone pan-European, an export to be truly ashamed of, as they weren't all English, by a long way. I jumped to my feet looking at my watch, said, 'Oh, my God,' and tore out of the room.

Back at the pleb's bar there was some indignation from the new pals but we had a couple of beers and depressed ourselves by talking about the game against Morocco. The consensus was that the people we felt most sorry for, except for ourselves, were the Moroccans. 'Imagine if it had been us that won and then we found out that the Norwegians had beaten Brazil,' said Kenny. We all nodded sombrely, contemplating horror once again.

With about fifteen minutes to departure, in rolled Bouncer, a very satisfied-looking man-mountain indeed. He held up his hand to forestall comment. 'A gentleman does not discuss these matters.' Kenny said, 'But you're just a big loon frae the Mearns, so you're going to, aren't ye?' Bouncer's eyes lit up, 'Oh aye, he said with relish, 'but I'm going to spin it oot a bit, like.'

As he started on his tale my attention was distracted by Buckets, now standing at the bar saying to the barman, 'Is this *Seize* for sale?' *Seize* is what they call Kronenbourg 1664 in France and Buckets went through the whole ritual again, cracking the staff up. A couple of the other lads had taken it up and Buckets was hatching another ploy, which I didn't find out about until we were queuing to get on the plane. The Club Class passengers were all led to the front so that they could get on first and Buckets manoeuvred our lot in behind them. He then started saying urgently to me, 'You are one rapacious bastard. You made nearly three hundred grand on that last deal! The most I can do on this is one mil one. The least you'll get is two hundred thou.' All this was in a kind of piercing whisper. He then said, 'Shhh!' to me as I gazed at him in fascinated disbelief and went on, 'These bastards are listening to every word,' indicating the people in front of us. And the ones that had heard him were straining their ears while pretending like crazy not to. He then leaned forward and whispered total gibberish into my ear and then leaned back and said, 'Okay, we'll talk on the plane. Where is your own plane, by the way? Still in Nice?'

There are times when my tongue leads a wild and carefree life of its own and Buckets' craziness was infectious. There was a fairly hefty lady standing right in front of us with the Club Class people, who was carrying three giant hat boxes, all prominently labelled with her name and destination. 'Siobhan,' I said, tapping her on the shoulder. 'Siobhan from Dublin! It's been ages. How have you been?' Siobhan hadn't a clue who I was but was game. 'Hello again,' she said, 'were you down at Longchamps? I'm just on my way over home for the meeting there.'

'That would explain the hats,' I gabbled. 'Yes,' she said. 'Such a nuisance but necessary still, I'm afraid.' I said, 'Oh yes, absolutely. Standards are standards.' I didn't even notice giving the woman at the desk my ticket and passport and getting them back because just as we got there and I said this Buckets lost it totally. He was laughing and laughing and laughing and I started as well, as by this time we had a hatbox each and a new friend in Siobhan, an awfully nice woman. We stowed her hat boxes for her and I found my seat, on the aisle as always. Buckets hissed, 'Talk to you later. Remember, one mil one total max,' and made his way to his own seat.

Once the plane had taken off I relaxed a bit. This was not just because I was on my way home to Blighty, home and beauty, for I still had the British Customs and Immigration, among the most stringent in the world, to get through, but because a stewardess came over saying, 'Dr –, Dr –.' and handed me a very nicely gift-wrapped half bottle of brandy. 'It is a gift from Madelaine,' she said, 'for your patience.' I went to open it.

'No, no,' she said, scoldingly, 'keep it for your patients,' and went and brought me a miniature of brandy. Every time my glass went down a quarter of an inch she brought another one, and by the time we got to London I wasn't worried about jail at all, or anything else for that matter, and even if I did get sussed, it would be a British jail. I've been in a French jail, only overnight, thank Christ (don't ask), and I don't recommend the experience for those of a nervous disposition, or even for those with nerves of steel.

The Club Class people were no longer glaring at me as I now, however incongruously dressed, seemed to be one of them. My tongue, it of the wild and free existence, took umbrage. 'Buckets,' it yelled, now in totally Bad Blackie mode, 'get your arse in here.' Buckets appeared, picking up his cue as though by telepathy. 'One mil, one fifty and I can't squeeze another Ecu out of them. They know you're in with me and they know you're on the heavy end. Deal?' I looked at him, keenly aware that we now had a small but deeply interested audience. 'Deal,' I said and spat a big one into my hand, holding it out. All credit to Buckets, his eyes widened only slightly and he spat into his own hand, said, 'Deal,' again and grasped mine firmly, then went on with a wink, 'Fuck all meat-eaters, eh?' I hadn't a clue what this was about but I said, 'And the vegetarians, too.' I then went on to tell Buckets about the McCartney kids at Linda's cremation asking, 'What's that lovely smell, Dad?' and watched the ripple of revulsion in the nearby seats.

Buckets then went back to his seat, turning at the curtain which, apart from centuries-old attitudes, is all that separates the plebs from the patricians, at least on this plane, to say again, 'Meat-eaters, eh?' with another complicit wink. After a minute or two I went up and joined him as he was telling Bouncer and Kenny what was going on. Bouncer was amazed. 'What kind of low profile do you call this?' he hissed. 'I've seen Oscar winners with lower profiles. Away back to your seat and sit quiet.'

So I did, but the slightly emphatic way I refused the inflight meal did cause a ripple of uneasiness among my nearby fellow Clubbers, some of whom followed my example, though they probably hadn't stuffed themselves with hot dogs in the airport bar, like I had. I hate eating on planes, all that having to tuck in your elbows and being squeezed-in and tidy.

I spent the rest of the journey in the mode I had originally planned, head in a book, my concentration broken only by the teenage girl beside me when she couped half a cup of hot coffee in my lap. It wasn't burning hot and the book and the plastic shelf caught most of it but she got her napkin and was just going to commence dabbing when I caught her eye and she realised that she was about to start scrubbing the pubic region of a slightly worrying old geezer in his fifties. I said that it was okay and she said, 'But it stains.' I said in my best avuncular Doctor manner, 'Lass, there are stains there that you don't even want to think about.' The older man in the window seat, whom I think might be her dad, laughed at this and she did too, but she was a bit too late to be convincing.

When we landed in London I was off well ahead of the rest of the lads and breezed through Immigration without turning a hair. The guy did quickly look at the picture and then at me but the differences didn't seem to register. If I were a terrorist I would travel Club Class because a lot of people went through on the nod, just waving their passports in front of him. I didn't have the nerve to do that even with the Dutch courage.

The reunion in the departure lounge for Scotland when the rest got there was great. There we were, seven or eight of us, the defeated homecomers of the Tartan Army, punching the air in glee and yelling, 'Yes!' The really great thing about it was that the day before I hadn't known any of these guys, but now we were a unit, just for a wee while, and my triumph in smuggling myself home was their triumph, too. Our last combined act of defiance of authority was for Bouncer to boost Kenny up on his shoulders to reach the telly in the centre of the hall and switch it from some soundless programme about Princess Di to coverage of the South Africa–Saudi game, complete with high-volume commentary. No one complained, though this may be because others of the Army had gathered around by now and were singing, 'Doctor, Doctor, give us a song, Doctor, give us a song.' Kenny turned the volume down and I sang 'The Freedom Come All Ye', the Hamish Henderson song that is my choice for our National Anthem, and which Pete the Prod and I had sung, faces tripping us, on the long way back into St Etienne after the game.

The Glasgow and Edinburgh shuttles were both delayed, mine by nearly two hours, so we were well sung out and I at least was well fou on the flight back up, of which I remember very little. I do remember, though, arriving back to the bosom of my family to be greeted by my wife with a sympathetic smile and the words, 'Oh hello love, did we not win?'

Well, we did win. We may have lost at the football, but the Tartan Army won, once again, the battle for the hearts of our hosts, and those of the world watching on TV. And I got to do something that grown-ups don't often get a chance to. I had an adventure.

Absolutely Sweet Maires

Plans change. Promises made sometimes can't be kept. I had thought that I, at the head of a troupe of fine actors, would be guesting George, John, Anne and the rest, plus our Dutch chums, all over France, but George's wife got very ill (she's now recovered), the play went financially about as far west as it could get without meeting itself on the way back round the planet, and Man U Mike had a major falling out with the Dutch, so I fell back on Plan B.

Plan B involved me blagging the money I had put away to pay my income tax and accepting with alacrity the offer of a lift from Tumshie and his partner, the lovely Blondes Have More Fun. I met them in Dover after the London footie fest and we got the ferry into sunshine, great wine and a straight road to Paris, where we had arranged to meet Pete the Prod. I will not soon forget the sight of a couple in one of those bosky laybys that the French do so well, dancing dreamily while looking into each other's eyes as the sun shone and their car stereo played 'Perfect Day'. As far as I was concerned it was a Perfect Start – and it got better. I successfully navigated us from the motorway into the centre of Paris and their hotel with nary a cross word exchanged. How easy can that be? I can't drive and I didn't know that I could read maps, but wonder of wonders, I suddenly turned into Mr Super Navigator. I then guided us all over France, including the wee toty roads with strange signposts, yet again without a cross word.

Pete, Tumshie and I had all been awarded a ticket for the Brazil game because of our attendance at overseas matches. I discovered that I had been vouchsafed mine when I was opening my mail on the Glasgow–Edinburgh train. The frequent travellers on the 8.30 a.m. probably talk still of the maniac who sprang to his feet, howled, 'Yes, Yes, Yes . . .' more times than Molly Bloom and then attempted to kiss everyone in the carriage, starting with a woman called Margaret who had the bad luck to be sitting across from me. I succeeded with Margaret, who seemed almost as chuffed as I was at my good fortune, but some of the guys got a bit miffed until I explained. Tickets were the first topic of conversation everywhere in France, but more of that later.

The people on the train tried not to look astonished at my being so delighted to be offered the chance to pay £135 just for a seat at a game of football and some of them even succeeded, but the forthright Margaret said, 'Are you daft, or are you made of money?' One out of two isn't bad, I thought, though at that point full awareness of the catastrophic nature of the play's losses had not yet dawned. I already knew I was daft.

So, ticket for the first game safely pouched, we are in Paris three days before the game starts. Did we eat brilliant food, drink the blood-red wine and meet old and new chums? Does Dolly Parton sleep on her back? The second morning I was there I was buying some pain au chocolat in a café when there was a tap on my shoulder. It was the Nutty Prof., Handy Andy himself at 8.30 in the morning and him still not returned to his hotel. 'I'm already up on the trip,' he told me, 'because I've still got most of the money and people I came with.' Then he was off to who knows what adventures, dressed in the full fig, his feathered bonnet bobbing and weaving between the two French people he was with as they did their boulevardier bit down what I can only describe as boulevards, smiling at the people they met and exuding bonhomie and beer fumes.

The Mayor of Paris was at the Brazil game, and so were several thousand people connected with his office. We didn't meet him but he had a lot of free tickets to distribute, as did the other maires in France but more of that later.

On the day of the game we got the train out to the centre of St Denis, a somewhat featureless wee ville in the Parisian suburbs, but one which had put its frilly knickers and garters on for the occasion, and which did its best to do us proud. I met Mahoney in the town square and he told me that Sweeney was off finding a street called the Avenue of Bobby Sands. I thought he was kidding but I met them again an hour or so later and they had both been there. What's more, they had found the equivalent of a French fish 'n' chicken bar in it and had bought a French chicken supper. They then collected a few other eejits and wandered up and down it singing, 'Could you go a chicken supper Bobby Sands?' Yesterday's sick joke becomes folklore – and from two Tims as well. They apparently received a serious talking to from a French gent who knew all about Bobby Sands and who thought that this was almost sacrilegious. 'He did have a point,' said Mahoney, 'but how were we to know that he would understand? You have to reach beyond hatred and bigotry for the laugh behind it.' I'm not sure I agree with him and I certainly wouldn't have done it, but they're closer to it than I am.

In the square, Del Amitri sang their dirge about us not coming home too soon as a London DJ exhorted the crowd with, 'Come on you Jocks, this is live radio,' and a whole lot of other frenetic crap. Whoever it was that was listening to it was soon unable to hear this voice as it was drowned in something you don't hear very often in the Tartan Army: the growling of several thousand bears and multiple choruses of a ditty, created for the occasion, which was 'Shitface, Shitface, get tae fuck. Shitface, get tae fuck.' My own favourite comment on the onstage scenario was from a Bellshill guy who turned his back, hoisted his kilt and stood like that until the stage emptied.

While we were having an extremely pleasant lunch just round the corner from the square prior to sauntering to the ground, smug in the knowledge that we had turned down an offer of £800 each for our tickets, Eck the Fish, which is what More Steam has christened him, stopped at our table for a chat. He probably prefers to be called Alex Salmond, as that is his given name, and a right pleasant and informative chat it was. He looked great in the old-fashioned Scotland jersey and there's something a bit old fashioned about his straight way of talking as well. I was mightily impressed by him and his two minders, one of whom looks like a twelve-year-old clone of the other, and he'll get my vote. Again. And again. Until we've won the right to be fighting among ourselves and not answerable to our southern cousins for our good behaviour.

As Tumshie, Blondes Have More Fun and I got to the ground, we encountered an obstacle in the shape of a youngish but very pompous *gendarme*. All of the polis in France are called Jean, I learned from Big Jed in St Remy, as in Jean-darme. By the time we got to St Etienne, the cops were introducing themselves as, '*Je m'appelle Jean – Gendarme.*' They thought it was hilarious and Jed deserves the credit for yet another friendly propaganda coup for the Tartan Army, as there are few more frightening humans than an angry French *flic*. But I digress once again.

This guy was guarding a 50-yard strip of pavement which he was keeping one-way, so that all the fat cats, like the mayor's hangers-on and the (literally) tens of thousands of Mastercard and other 'corporate guests' would have a clear road to the best seats in the house. This, according to the Jean, meant that we had to walk round the entire Stade de France to get that 50-yard distance. Tumshie does not react well to official stupidity and, as his eyes narrowed and his jaw set, I prepared for trouble. But the cop realised that we weren't going anywhere, and as Tumshie kept demanding on what authority he was blocking the pavement, he suddenly pretended that we didn't exist and took to stopping other people as we drifted past him, pulling a few more lads with us.

The people we were passing though were seriously rich – fur coats, diamonds, high heels – and that was just the men – and not a scarf or a rickety between them. I've never seen this at a game before and I hope I never do again because a consequence was that they all sat on their hands during the game because they didn't give a stuff who won, even if they did know who was playing, and the atmosphere in the huge stadium was leaden, except for the comparatively few Brazilians and Scots. We tried our best, but it was like shouting into a vacuum, and the game itself didn't help.

On our way in, as we queued and then queued again to be patted down and frisked by the thousands of French punters hired to protect the Brazilians and the Scots from each other, I got talking to Alan, a guy from Falkirk who was just in front of me and trembling uncontrollably with excitement. It transpired that he hadn't had a ticket but had come anyway and was mooching forlornly about when a Frenchman came up and sold him a top-class ticket at face value. Alan said: 'I think he could see that I was in despair. He just asked if I wanted a ticket and then handed it over. I don't think he even wanted any money at first but I made him take it. He even tried to give me about thirty francs change. That's two big favours I owe the next French person I meet. I always try to double the favours if I can.' A good deed goes around the world, as they say, and Alan tries to make sure of this by sending one each way.

I met him in the soft-drinks queue at half-time, as he was sitting quite near us and it transpired that he was sitting beside the guy who gave him the ticket. 'I think he's saying his wife couldn't come, or something,' said Alan, 'but jeez-o, what a good guy.' I organised a mini storm of applause for him when we went back up and the *gentilhomme* stood up and took a bow, giving us the thumbs up, Alan's scarf around his neck by this time, the newest of new recruits to the legions of light, aka the Tartan Army.

All the stuff about segregation turned out to be nonsense, as we were seated beside a big block of Brazilians, the security being one old guy well into his sixties who was supposed to be guarding an aisle about forty yards long. Pete and I got a respectful nod and smile from him for singing all the words to the 'Marseillaise' when they played it at the start. I learned them for the trip, but Pete the Prod, who isn't a Prod at all but a film producer, knew them already and is really brilliant at singing it, a fact which was to prove highly advantageous later on.

The Brazilians were pretty quiet during the game, and they, as well as us, were pretty disappointed at the result. Who would have thought at that point that the Scottish defence, renowned for its minginess, would let in two goals like those? But the Brazilians had expected to humiliate us and they hadn't, so their supporters were glum. Pete and I tried to get them going – 'Sing when you're winning, you don't even sing when you're winning' – but it was a bit of an anticlimax all round at the ground. It was different at the Brazilian village when we went to pick up Blondes HMF. When we got there it was absolutely lashing with rain and there she was, soaked to the skin and smashed, smiling beatifically at the mud-soaked madmen dancing in the rain. One of the acts was a troupe of Brazilian transvestites and they were excellent. I was standing watching them beside a family group from Aberdeen, whose aged patriarch was watching them through narrowed eyes. After a couple of minutes he abruptly announced, 'Ay, I'm right. Eyes aff them. They're loons,' and dragged his party away. I met some of the transvestites on the way back into Paris on the train, something which I have lived to regret, as while I and a lot of others were singing, 'Get your balls out for the lads,' I found myself between a couple of the dancing queens, being kissed by them. Blondes HMF, it turns out, was doing her paparazzi number with her camera and the snaps she took have been duly circulated round the chums to much hilarity and ribald speculation.

If Paris was a moveable feast, then Bordeaux was a veritable banquet. The troops were a bit dispersed in Paris because it's so big and so expensive, but Bordeaux, home of *le vignoble bordelais*, is compact enough to allow big parties to form, and form they did, as the wine was cheap and the people cheerful. I met an Albion Rovers supporter in one of the major party areas who was carrying a bottle of Buckfast. When I remarked on this he said, 'I keep filling it up with French stuff but it was empty when I left Coatbridge. I just brought it to annoy folk like you.'

It's difficult to convey the sheer intensity of the enjoyment and of the interactions between the Norwegians, the Scots and the people of Bordeaux. They had set up a tented village, with tents for all of the countries playing there, selling food and drink till the small hours. It was in a square called *Place des Quinconces* (I looked it up in my French dictionary and it says 'quincunx'; you can look that up for yourself), and it was a bit like being in a zoo at first while the Norwegians and Scots danced and drank together, the Bordeaux folk strolled past at a distance, peering at the barbarians a bit apprehensively. The deputy mayor of Bordeaux told me that his people are 'more bourgeois than the bourgeois' and very reserved. He said that they are renowned for it, but by the end of day one in Bordeaux you could have fooled me, as they were in there giving it laldy with the rest of us. Alain, the deputy mayor, said that he was amazed at their reaction. 'You even have us talking to each other. This is most unusual and very enjoyable for all of us.' When we left the morning after the game the local newspaper had a headline saying 'MISSING YOU ALREADY', which was a compliment to both nations. High passions and national fervour on both sides, with not a blow struck or even a harsh word exchanged, as far as I could tell.

My second favourite quote from Bordeaux was from a Scot to a Norwegian. They were both standing peeing against one of those giant oblong wheelie bins that keep the towns so tidy in France, both in their total regalia, feathered bonnet on one side, horned helmet on the other. The Scottish guy looked up just as he was dropping his kilt and saw the Norwegian, who was just finishing fastening his leggings. 'Hey, pal,' said the Scot, reaching over the bin, 'hands across the watter, eh?' The Norwegian got the joke and went off roaring to tell his friends. I was laughing so much I dropped the bottles of beer I was carrying.

My favourite quote, though, was from Alain. It was, 'Yes, I have a ticket for you.' I was an official guest of the Maire of Bordeaux at a dinner (it's a long story) and Pete had blagged his way onto the guest list as well. Tickets for the game were going for hundreds of pounds but we had discovered that the *maires* of each city had tickets in their fist for giving away as hospitality. Call me a fat cat because when I found this out I didn't tell anybody but Pete. The dinner was superb, as were the wines, and I'd already been told by Alain that I had a ticket, but Pete didn't have one yet, as he wasn't on the official guest list. We were both standing talking to Brian Wilson, Her Majesty's Minister for Tons of Things, whom we both know, but didn't know the other did, and Pete kept trying to bring up the subject that one of Brian's pals – i.e., him – was at that moment in time a ticket-free zone. Brian, however, was full of the joys. 'We'll need to sing something for them,' he kept saying. 'Let's do "Bandiera Rossa".' I accused him of being geographically challenged, as this is an Italian song, and he said, 'The "Internationale", let's do that.' None of us knew the French words and it seemed to me a bit insulting to sing it in English, as it was composed in France and in French in 1871. Then Pete had his brainwave. He walked to the far side of the room, where the other performers had been, and nodded to Brian, who clapped his hands for attention and pointed to Pete. He started, in full voice, and he's a good singer, *'Allons enfants de la patrie,'* and sang the 'Marseillaise'. He was a sight to see, standing there in his kilt and blouson shirt, singing the only national anthem in the world that raises the hair on the necks of other nationals, including me, and giving it absolute yeehah. After the applause, Alain came up and asked if it might be possible to borrow Pete's kilt for the game the next day. Pete, with a slight gulp, did the hospitable thing and agreed, and Alain said, 'You wish a ticket for the game beside your friend, *non?*' like the politician that he is, and the deal was done.

Pete's killer-diller negotiation, however, was on the day after the game, when he went to pick up his kilt from Alain. Now armed with the knowledge that the *maire* of St Etienne had tickets to give away, he asked Alain, as one kilt wearer to another, if he would phone M'sieu Michel Thiollière and get us a couple of briefs. *'Pas de problème'* said your *homme* and did so on the spot.

Being the paranoid people that we are, we didn't believe it was going to happen and when we got to St Etienne my first move was to insinuate myself into a visiting cultural delegation of Highlanders and Islanders and introduce myself to Michel the *maire*. He's a professor of English who writes about football and when I said hello and presented him with a copy of the very tome you are holding, version one, he invited me to come and read some of the stories at several cultural dos in the cafés in the town centre. I agreed with alacrity, as that was what he wanted to hear, but I confess that the idea of reading to the bear pit in the Bar Glasgow, especially if half of them were French intellectuals, did not fill me with thrilled anticipation, especially as it was scheduled for two hours before kick-off.

Michel, God love him, then asked me if I had a ticket, so that deal was now belt and braces, or kilt and trews. I didn't have the brass neck to follow through on that, as Pete got the two promised tickets, and I phoned the office to tell them I wouldn't need any more. On reflection I shouldn't have, as I could have given one to any number of footsoldiers on the march up to the Stade Geoffroy-Buichard. If you weren't on that march, I'm not even going to try to tell you about it, except to say that it was the high point in my Tartan Army career so far. I thought my heart was going to burst with pride as we chanted and cheered our way through the applauding citizens of St Etienne. I may have perjured my immortal soul to get there, but if that's the price, I'll pay it gladly for that hour.

Dylan says, in 'Absolutely Sweet Marie'; 'To live outside the law you must be honest,' and now I have been, so thank you, Absolutely Sweet *Maires*. Suas Alba!